Ramsgate

The town and its seaside heritage

Historic England

Ramsgate

The town and its seaside heritage

Geraint Franklin, with Nick Dermott and Allan Brodie

Historic England

thanet
district council

  THE RAMSGATE SOCIETY

Front cover
A view of Ramsgate harbour and clock house, with the sea lapping against the slipways.
[DP247126]

Inside front cover
This 1960s view of the Marina Bathing Pool was taken by postcard photographer John Hinde. Behind the modernist café building can be seen Granville Marina, the former Établissement *and the Edwardian cliff lift. The pool was infilled in the 1980s.*
[John Hinde Archive / John Hinde Collection]

Frontispiece
This recent aerial photograph, taken from the south-east, shows the curved piers of the 18th-century harbour, adjoined by Ramsgate Sands to the west and the modern port to the east. The railway line and Margate Road can clearly be made out in the distance.
[33061/004, Damian Grady]

Inside back cover
Steps leading from Albion Place Gardens, landscaped with Pulhamite artificial rockwork, to Albion Hill and Albion Place.
[DP251116]

Back cover
The west pier and lighthouse, with the seafront terraces of the west cliff in the distance.
[DP251302]

Published by Liverpool University Press on behalf of Historic England, The Engine House, Fire Fly Avenue, Swindon SN2 2EH
www.HistoricEngland.org.uk

Historic England is a Government service championing England's heritage and giving expert, constructive advice.

© Historic England 2020

The views expressed in this book are those of the authors and not necessarily those of Historic England.

Images (except as otherwise shown) © Historic England Archive; Figs 36, 38, 41, 47, 48, 52 and 89 are reproduced by permission of Historic England Archive; Figs 92 and 105 are © Historic England Archive. Aerofilms Collection; Map 1 on p 150 and Map 2 on p 153 are based on Ordnance Survey data © Crown Copyright and database right 2020, Ordnance Survey Licence Number 100024900.

First published 2020

ISBN 978-1-78962-189-1

British Library Cataloguing in Publication data
A CIP catalogue record for this book is available from the British Library.

Application for the reproduction of images should be made to Historic England. Every effort has been made to trace the copyright holders and we apologise in advance for any unintentional omissions, which we would be pleased to correct in any subsequent edition of this book.

For more information about images from the Archive, contact Archives Services Team, Historic England, The Engine House, Fire Fly Avenue, Swindon SN2 2EH; telephone (01793) 414600.

Typeset in Georgia Pro Light 9.25/13pt

Page layout by Carnegie Book Production
Printed in the Czech Republic via Akcent Media Limited.

Contents

Acknowledgements

This book is based on fieldwork and research conducted by Geraint Franklin. The final chapter was prepared by Nick Dermott of Thanet District Council and Allan Brodie of Historic England. Clive Aslet is thanked for writing the foreword. The location maps were prepared by Geraint Franklin. Perhaps the most valuable contribution was made by Chris Redgrave who was responsible for the new photography. Other photographers and those who supplied images are acknowledged in the captions.

I would like to thank my colleagues at Historic England for their help and support. My greatest debt is to Allan Brodie, who has been an unstinting source of seaside expertise and good humour over the course of the project. He edited the text, which has also benefited from the comments of Nick Dermott and Jonathan Kewley. Martyn Barber, Wayne Cocroft, Peter Kendall, Rebecca Lane, Jonathan Last and Fiona Small provided valuable insights and comments. The support of past and present colleagues Susie Barson, Michael Bellamy, Simon Buteux, Marion Brinton, James O Davies, Sarah Gibson, Pete Herring, Dave Hooley, John Hudson, Liz Pollard, Martin Small and Rob Lloyd Sweet is gratefully acknowledged. I would also like to thank the team at Liverpool University Press, including Alison Welsby, Catherine Pugh and Patrick Brereton, along with Rachel Chamberlain at Carnegie Book Production.

Members of the Ramsgate Heritage Action Zone partnership team, especially programme manager Louisa Hrabowy, are thanked for their enthusiasm and cooperation. The interest and support of John Walker, David Gullick and their colleagues at the Ramsgate Society is gratefully acknowledged. Catriona Blaker, Brian Daubney, Stephen Davis, Edward Diestelkamp, Christopher Garrand, Gerald Hyland and Benedict Kelly have shared their insights into aspects of Ramsgate's history, while Melissa Conway and colleagues at Land Use Consultants provided access to research undertaken for their historic characterisation study. Michael Child, Ralph Hoult and Phil Spain are thanked for providing historic photographs and illustrations.

Access to St George's Church, Chatham House School, Chilton Farmhouse and Townley House was kindly provided by Jennifer Smith, Chris Freeman, Nigel Phethean and Ivan del Renzio respectively, while I would like to thank the many owners who welcomed me into their historic homes. Thanks are due to the staff of Canterbury Cathedral Archives, Historic England Archives and Library, Kent History and Library Centre, Margate and Ramsgate libraries, the Montefiore Endowment, the National Archive and the National Army Museum. Lastly, I am particularly grateful to Sally and Rob Holden for making available their collection of historic documents and photographs.

Geraint Franklin

Foreword

Recently a sticker has appeared on the window of our house in Ramsgate. A neighbour put it there as part of an admirable Historic England initiative to interest local people in their past. There's a sticker for every house in the street, or Lawn, as we call it, detailing an individual who once lived there. Our chosen occupant, at the turn of the 20th century, was a butcher, Thomas Stroud. One of his four children, Frederick, was killed on the Somme during the First World War. Ramsgate was a place of independent tradesmen, who have, when demanded, done their bit. Next door to us lives Bob Pryor, who leads walks describing Ramsgate's role during the Second World War. Bombing, for a town so close to the Continent, was such a danger that air raid shelters were formed out of tunnels in the chalk cliffs.

Mr Stroud would have been in our house when the library that we see from our front room was built. It is a festive piece of classicism, with a cupola and the Ramsgate coat of arms over the door. The original collections were destroyed when an arsonist attempted to burn it down in 2004. But wartime photographs exist in the library at Margate, showing a policeman in white sleeves calmly directing traffic in the town, above a notice which reads 'Enemy Shelling in Progress'. It was from Ramsgate harbour that the famous 'little ships' sailed to relieve Dunkirk. In an earlier period, Ramsgate was a port from which soldiers embarked for the Napoleonic Wars.

That is about as far as Ramsgate's story goes, in terms of national events. This splendid book tells a different tale. Largely, it is the transformation of a modest fishing village into a seaside resort in the Georgian and Victorian periods, followed, in the second half of the 20th century, by a decline in fortune as holidaymakers deserted England's south coast for warmer shores and, to make matters worse, the Kentish

coalmines closed. Geraint Franklin's research has been formidable. I can only add a few addenda based on my own experience of life in this Monte Carlo of Thanet, whose topography of west cliff, east cliff and 18th-century harbour would be famous, if only it were located on the Côte d'Azur.

'All London quits London', wrote the anonymous author of *All About Ramsgate and Broadstairs* in 1865: 'the old broken case remains, but the works and moving figures are taken out. Russell Square sends its plate to the banker's, and, leaving word that it is on the Continent, bargains for a first-floor and double-bedded rooms at Ramsgate'. The seaside community began its migration to other quarters, vacating the best rooms in their houses for visitors:

> Those virtuous elderly spinsters who have lived the long winter months in their deserted houses, solitary as spiders in their webs, wake up from their torpidity and grow lively with the summer heat. They take from the linen-closet the clean blinds for the bedroom windows and the net curtains for the handsome drawing rooms and 'neat parlours'; the faded chintz sofa-coverings are washed and ironed, and, buying a bottle of furniture polish, they make their poor arms ache with rubbing up the dull tables and sideboards into a waxy lustre.

In 1842, *Punch* described Ramsgate as a town of cannibals. The inhabitants fed themselves off 'lodgers caught in the season ... half-a-dozen single men are found quite sufficient to feed a widow and a child or two for a year, if subsisting in a moderate way; whilst the more luxurious eaters – the owners of drawing and sitting-rooms – require husbands, wives and families'. Our Mr Stroud may also have feasted off visitors during the summer months; everybody who could provide rooms seemed to. (And not only during the summer months: October was regarded with particular favour when the poet Samuel Taylor Coleridge came with his doctor, the only problem being that the sea had, by then, warmed to sybaritic temperatures – 'not cold enough to my liking').

Our house was built in the year of the *Punch* article quoted above. As Franklin reveals, there was a nasty accident when the street, Guildford Lawn, was being built, fortunately not fatal; a labourer fell from a collapsing scaffold and William Saxby, son of the builder, also called William, only saved himself by grabbing the gutter, from which he hung for some time. We live with an accident of a different sort – one of planning – since the Saxbys could not make Guildford Lawn into a crescent, only a dog's leg, with our house in the angle. As a result, it has a very narrow frontage, from which the house behind it expands like a wedge of cheese. The back is therefore considerably wider than the front, and the little garden wider still; for some unexplained reason, the sash windows on this side are enormous, even in the first-floor bedroom. There are few back gardens in Ramsgate, only urban yards. Our small garden is therefore regarded as an exceptional luxury, which only falls to us because at some point in the past an occupant got hold of the land containing the communal well. When it was built, all the houses in the terrace would have drawn their water from it. Originally, the space that is now occupied by flower beds would have been covered by sheds. One of them presumably housed the privy.

The style of Guildford Lawn is what used to be called Quality Street; after the 1901 play by J M Barrie, whose original production boasted stage sets by Edwin Lutyens. It has a stucco façade and a bow front: exactly the sort of architecture – flashy and, because the stucco was intended to look like stone, while hiding any shins in the underlying brickwork, 'sham' – that would have infuriated A W N Pugin, who mortified himself by building The Grange on the edge of a town of which he greatly disapproved. Guildford Lawn is one of a number of lawns in Ramsgate, of which the prettiest is Liverpool Lawn; no other town chose to name streets in this way and it is not quite clear what a lawn, in this context, actually was. Obviously, though, it involved grass. Our grass disappeared at the turn of the 20th century when it was replaced by a terrace of 'villas'. From the balcony at the top of the house, there is a distant view of the sea.

In Mr Stroud's time, Ramsgate was booming. Locally there is considerable nostalgia for the golden age of the seaside holiday. With the economic catastrophe of the 1970s and 1980s came deprivation: beyond the pretty facades of the old town lie debt, poverty, low educational achievement and other indicators of deprivation. There is now a tentative revival. The signs appear, year by year, in the shops and restaurants, which are clearly serving a more prosperous clientele. Ramsgate is still beyond comfortable commuting distance of London but it suits the increasing number of people who do not need to be at their desks every day. This includes the creatives – photographers, designers, writers – who respond to the architecture and topography, and are pleased to find that house prices are still relatively cheap.

The opening of the Turner Contemporary art gallery in 2011 created a 'Margate effect', some of which has spilled over. Its rejuvenating power is not felt equally. Local people are apt to disparage the DFL (Down from London) crowd. But they are creating work. Good builders have never been so busy, due to the (by Ramsgate standards) giddy amounts of money being spent on the doing-up of old property. In 1964, the Ramsgate

Society was founded in response to an outrageous attempt to demolish some of the harbour buildings that threatened the identity of the town. It's difficult to imagine that happening now. The quality of restoration celebrated by the design awards given twice yearly by the Ramsgate Heritage and Design Forum is impressive.

It could yet go wrong. If Kent International Airport at Manston were to reopen, as some would like, as a cargo airport served by night flights, the Ramsgate renaissance will be knocked on the head. Horribly out of kilter with modern thinking, the Westwood Cross Shopping Centre has arisen with little apparent regard for the infrastructure that serves it – a poor omen for the large number of new houses that are projected for Thanet. But the balance, I believe, is tipping in favour of a bright future, based on quality of life and the charm of Ramsgate's built heritage. How timely it is that the town's architecture should be celebrated in this excellent book. As part of Ramsgate's Heritage Action Zone, it will help to make the town's colourful past play an important role in its future.

Clive Aslet
President, Ramsgate Society

1

Introduction

Due to its outward-facing position Ramsgate grew from a fishing village within the parish of St Lawrence to a harbour of refuge for shipping anchored in the Downs and a prosperous port. At the same time as the renewal of the harbour was getting underway in the 1750s, the town was gaining a reputation as a sea-bathing resort. The latter was in one sense dependent on the former: Ramsgate Sands had accumulated against the pier that preceded the 18th-century harbour. The contrast between those wealthy, health-conscious visitors and the rough-and-ready, vernacular appearance of the seafaring settlement must have diminished with the construction of terraces, squares and crescents along with assembly rooms, libraries and saltwater baths for the 'fashionable company'. The Regency period could be regarded as Ramsgate's golden era: aristocrats and the gentry flocked to the resort, while royal patronage conferred respectability and prestige.

The town's population rose steadily throughout the 19th century as new and affordable modes of transport – the hoy (a small sailing boat adapted to carry passengers), the steam boat and later the train – brought a newly mobile middle class. A seaside guide of 1846 pronounced that 'of the three watering places in the Isle of Thanet, Ramsgate is considered as the most fashionable, Margate as the most lively and bustling, Broadstairs as the most quiet and retired'.[1] But as Charles Dickens's 'The Tuggs's at Ramsgate' (1836) and William Frith's painting *Ramsgate Sands* (1851–5) attest, the resort's exclusive reputation was already giving way to a bustling, heterogeneous character that combined class-consciousness with commercialisation. New facilities and seafront improvements signalled civic pride while serving a growing resident population (Fig 1).

Although Ramsgate was eclipsed by Margate as a lower middle-class and working-class destination, novel entertainments and attractions continued to draw holidaymakers for much of the 20th century. But wartime damage and post-war austerity signalled a change in the town's fortunes, with the closure or stagnation of some of its attractions and facilities. As the national economy picked up, people enjoyed greater affluence and mobility, choosing to holiday abroad and spend their leisure time on day trips and short breaks rather than the traditional week at the seaside. Like most seaside resorts, Ramsgate began to be perceived as outdated and run-down. As local investment and job opportunities dried up, the decline of the town's small trades and industrial concerns threw

Painting a tug dry docked on the patent slipway. [DP247121]

Figure 1
Ramsgate's multi-layered maritime landscape. This view shows the 18th-century inner basin, Military Road, the Sailors' Home and Church, Smack Boys' Home and the arches of Royal Parade. Above, on the west cliff, are the seafront terraces of Nelson Crescent and Prospect Terrace.
[DP247152]

what had been a mixed economy off-balance. Potential directions were indicated by the conversion of the inner harbour basin to a marina and by a new ferry terminal, but by the early 21st century Ramsgate faced socio-economic problems and a poor self-image.

It was in response to these challenges that in March 2017 Ramsgate was chosen as one of the first tranche of ten Heritage Action Zones (HAZ). Delivered through a partnership including Historic England, Thanet District Council, Ramsgate Town Council, the Ramsgate Society and the Ramsgate Coastal Community Team, the initiative aims to stimulate economic growth and engage the local community by using Ramsgate's historic environment as a catalyst. Funding includes repair grants for listed buildings, scheduled monuments and registered parks and gardens, and capacity-building grants for wider area-based schemes. Training sessions have helped local volunteers to assess the significance of historic places, including carrying out character appraisals of Ramsgate's conservation areas. The environmental consultancy Land Use Consultants was commissioned to assess and map patterns of historic character across Ramsgate and its adjacent seascape.[2]

Historic England is contributing its own expertise to provide advice, support and understanding. So far, a total of 10 buildings have been added to the National Heritage List for England (NHLE), one existing list entry upgraded and a further ten list entries have been amended. Historic England's architectural investigators have completed a historic area assessment, using documentary research and fieldwork to explain the character and significance of Ramsgate's historic environment. Its aerial investigation and mapping team has analysed visible archaeological remains as they appear on historic and present-day aerial photographs.[3] Finally, Historic England's archaeologists have reviewed archaeological excavation reports to help form a more complete picture of prehistoric Ramsgate.[4]

This book represents another contribution to the Ramsgate Heritage Action Zone. It tells the story of the town's maritime and seaside heritage and charts its development over the past three centuries. It is a story that continues to unfold: the final chapter, contributed by Nick Dermott and Allan Brodie, takes up some of the town's contemporary challenges and examines the role that Ramsgate's past can play in guiding its future.

This town has something very singular, one notices the sea in everything.

Vincent Van Gogh, letter of 6 May 1876[5]

2 Origins and hinterland

Early Ramsgate

Ramsgate is a coastal settlement on the Isle of Thanet, at the easternmost tip of Kent. Around 8,000BC sea levels rose, causing Thanet to be cut off from mainland Kent by the Wantsum Channel, a navigable strait which was once crossed by ferry at the landlocked port of Sarre. If, as archaeologists have speculated, the Wantsum constituted a major prehistoric maritime route, then it follows that the Isle of Thanet likely represented an important trading and military gateway. Between Cliffsend at Pegwell Bay and Grenham Bay at Birchington-on-Sea, Thanet's coastline is formed of stretches of chalk cliff cut at intervals by gaps or 'gates' running down to the sea. Ramsgate is located at one; so too are Dumpton Gap, Broadstairs, Joss Bay, Botany Bay and Margate. These coves or valleys in the chalk offered a way down to the sea, sources of fresh water and shelter from the elements, suggesting early (although not necessarily extensive or continuous) settlement.

The names *Remmesgate* and *Remisgat* are first recorded in 1275; these are probably a compound of the Old English *hræfn*, raven and *geat*, gate. It originated as a fishing settlement, with a handful of fishermen's cottages, a pier to lay up boats, a few storehouses, and not much else. In John Lewis's 1723 account Ramsgate 'consist[ed] of a few houses and those poorly and meanly built'.[6] Little if any evidence survives of these early, impermanent dwellings but it is likely that they were built of materials that lay readily to hand. Flint and chalk were easily obtained from the foot of the cliffs, while timber was imported by sea for building boats and the pier structures. Thatch was available from the surrounding corn fields, and the thatched roofs of houses surrounding the harbour were still within living memory in 1885. Although one guidebook observed that the rural cottages and field walls were constructed of chalk, more substantial structures were probably timber framed.[7] The earliest surviving example is the late 14th or early 15th-century tithe barn at Ozengell Grange, one of the monastic granges of St Augustine's Abbey, Canterbury.

This map of c 1610, based on a plan by John Rogers of c 1548, shows the Isle of Thanet in relation to Sandwich, Richborough Castle, the River Stour and St Mary's Church at Reculver. To the right is depicted the Wantsum Channel, with annotations suggesting that parts were 'stopped' and 'now plain ground'. A curved wooden pier adjoins the settlements at Ramsgate, Broadgate and Margate. At the bottom left is the North Foreland, the headland which marks the boundary between the Thames Estuary and the southern North Sea. North is at the bottom of the map.
[British Library, London, UK © British Library Board. All Rights Reserved / Bridgeman Images]

John Leland, writing in the reign of Henry VIII, remarked on the lack of tree cover on Thanet, but local place names such as Southwood, Northwood, Westwood, Woodchurch and Birchington suggest that once there were trees, probably cleared to increase the tillage. Once trees became scarce, inhabitants became dependent on seaborne supplies of fuel and lumber. The northern and eastern parts of Thanet are characterised by relatively open, unenclosed fields, interspersed with hamlets and clusters of cottages. Early travellers noted the fertility of the well-drained chalky loams that yielded good arable crops of wheat and barley. Clover, alfalfa, sainfoin and canary grass were cultivated in the 18th century; elsewhere seeds of radish, spinach, mustard and cabbage were collected for the London market. Fennel, rosemary and thyme grew wild in quantity, while seaweed was used as manure and burnt to make potash.

However, corn dominated the agricultural economy. Ten windmills were recorded in 1719, of which two were located in the parish of St Lawrence. They were post mills, an early type where the mill structure pivots on a central post to catch the wind. Thanet grain was shipped out to London and the home market. Visiting Thanet in 1823, William Cobbett noted that 'the labourers' houses, all along through this island, [are] beggarly in the extreme. The people dirty, poor-looking; ragged, but particularly dirty'. He concluded that 'the richer the soil, and the more destitute of woods; that is to say, the more purely a corn country, the more miserable the labourers'.[8]

About 1.5km inland was Ramsgate's parish church of St Laurence, the focus of a high street and a rural settlement (Fig 2). The parish, spelt St Lawrence, contained about 141 householders in the reign of Edward I (1272–1307). St Laurence originated as one of three chapels of ease attached to St Mary at Minster in Thanet, which in turn was assigned to St Augustine's Abbey in 1124. It acquired its own parish in 1275, when its churchyard was consecrated for burial by the Archbishop of Canterbury. The widely coursed flintwork in the nave west wall is of possible early Norman date, while the arcaded tower and aisled nave were added in the late 12th century (Fig 3). The chancel was enlarged in the early 13th century. A short distance to the east was a medieval chantry chapel dedicated to the Holy Trinity, endowed with local land and possibly associated with the adjoining Ellington estate. After the Reformation it was converted into a dwelling and gradually fell into ruin (Fig 4).

It was adjoined by a timber-framed chantry house of probable 16th century date which survived until 1892.

Ramsgate and the sea

Key to the development of the harbour at Ramsgate was its strategic position on the eastern coast of Kent, looking out over the southern North Sea towards France and the Low Counties. To the north is the North Foreland, the gateway to the Thames Estuary and the port of London beyond. To the south lie the Downs, a roadstead or area of sea which provided anchorage, sheltered by the Goodwin Sands, a treacherous sandbank 16km in length. Beyond lies the Strait of Dover, one of the busiest seaways in the world. Not only was Ramsgate able to ply trade with London and the Continent; it also provided a safe haven for vessels driven from the Downs by storms.

The vill or township of Ramsgate was associated with the Cinque Ports as a limb or associate of Sandwich by 1354, when it was described as 'recently granted'.[9] As a corporate member, Ramsgate lay within the civil jurisdiction (or 'liberty') of Sandwich, being separated from the civil parish of St Lawrence by a boundary and right of way named the Liberty Way. More serious crimes were heard at the quarter sessions held at Sandwich, while minor offences would have been heard by the justices of the peace resident there. Ramsgate's right to levy dues upon vessels entering the harbour and their cargoes was confirmed at appeal in 1578 and 1616.

Writing between 1539 and 1543, Leland noted Ramsgate's 'smaul peere for shyppis'.[10] Early maps depict this as a curved timber pier extending from a quay, known as the Waterside, at the foot of the east cliff. It was equipped with a slipway at the end of Harbour Street. This area was known as the Corner or the Change, the latter possibly denoting an exchange or trading place. The pier was built by Ramsgate fishermen to lay up and fit out their vessels, and was maintained by rates or *droits* collected by locally elected pier wardens. In 1715 the structure was lengthened and by 1736 it had gained five groynes on the seaward side which trapped sediment and protected the pier foot from erosion. The old harbour was small, and dry at low water, so that although it could accommodate 40 vessels, ships of over 200 tons could only safely enter or leave

Figure 2
Thatched cottages are visible in this mid-19th-century view of St Lawrence High Street.
[DP251321; courtesy of Sally and Rob Holden]

Figure 3
The parish church of St Laurence, described in 1723 as 'a handsome building of field stones rough casted over as the rest of the churches in this island [of Thanet]' (Lewis 1723, 126).
[DP247299]

Figure 4
An 1817 engraving of the ruined chantry chapel of the Holy Trinity, which stood at the top of Grange Road. [DP251294; courtesy of Sally and Rob Holden]

Remains of an ancient Chapel, at St Lawrence, Thanet

the harbour at high tide. In 1566, 70 seamen, 25 houses and 14 boats ranging from 3 to 16 tonnes were recorded at Ramsgate. Comparison with Margate's 60 seamen, 108 houses and 15 boats and Broadstairs's 40 seamen, 98 houses and eight boats confirms that Elizabethan Ramsgate remained a fisherman's hamlet.

In 1586 the topographer and antiquarian William Camden observed that the inhabitants of Margate, Ramsgate and Broadstairs were 'excessively industrious, getting their living like amphibious animals both by sea and land'. Depending on the time of year 'they make nets, catch codd, herrings and mackerel, &c. make trading voyages, manure their land, plough, sow, harrow, reap, and store their corn, expert in both professions'.[11] John Lewis, writing in 1723, explained how the coastal workforce coordinated fishing with agricultural labour. The mackerel and herring fishing seasons, which lasted from May to July and from October to

November, were traditionally fitted around spring sowing, summer harvest and winter threshing. But such a division of labour did not long survive the agricultural revolution. Much of the catch was conveyed from Ramsgate to London, while barrelled herring were exported from the 1690s.

Ramsgate fishermen also ventured further afield. Two voyages were made each year to the North Sea to catch whiting and herring, the latter returning in time for the summer harvest. By the mid-18th century, between two and seven Thanet vessels with crews of more than 10 men sailed for Iceland, landing their catch of cod directly in London and at the northern ports. Fishing affected the entire community. Some fishing vessels were jointly owned, and longer voyages were financed by local farmers in return for a share of the profits. A celebration was traditionally held at the harbour on Shrove Tuesday to celebrate the safe return of the mariners. The risks of a seafaring life may help to explain the establishment in 1776 of a Ramsgate Society for the Benefit of Widows. This was probably a form of annuity society which offered a form of pension income for the buyer's wife in the event she became a widow.

During the 17th century Ramsgate became an established maritime trading centre. By 1701 it was the base for 45 vessels with a combined crew of 388 and a capacity of 4,100 tons, a greater number than any other Kentish port and ranked fifteenth in England. Aside from fishing, there were imports of coal from Newcastle and Sunderland, Norwegian timber and mixed cargoes from Rotterdam and Ostend. However, the port's competitive advantage lay not so much in its trading capacity but in the skills and mercantile interests of Ramsgate ship owners, captains, pilots, mariners, chandlers and boat builders. From the late 17th century, Ramsgate vessels traded with Russia and the Baltic, bringing cargoes of timber and hemp to the Thames naval dockyards at Chatham, Woolwich and Deptford. North America, the Caribbean and the Mediterranean were also on their sailing routes. On the proceeds of maritime commerce were erected several grand houses, some sporting elaborately shaped gables.

Ramsgate's mariners were also employed in safely piloting larger vessels to the Thames, assisting vessels in distress and bringing provisions to vessels anchored at the Downs. These services, known successively as 'foying' (perhaps derived from *voye*, the French word for way) and 'hovelling' (possibly named after fishermen's huts or hovels), are commemorated in the names of the former

Foy Boat Tavern on Sion Hill and the Hovelling Boat Inn on York Street. Camden noted that Thanet sailors 'are wont to bestir themselves lustily in recovering both ships, men, and marchandise endangered', a role which combined rescue with potentially lucrative salvage operations.[12] Thanet's gaps, sea caves and tunnels were exploited by smugglers, while contraband was also concealed in vessels entering the harbour.

Auxiliary trades developed around the harbour. From an early date the foreshore was used by those building and repairing fishing smacks for the Ramsgate fleet. The manufacture of rope, cables and sailcloth provided an alternative source of employment for seamen and their dependents. By the early 18th century two ropewalks extended west from High Street along the course of Cannon Street and George Street. Along these narrow alleyways thick threads of hemp were spun and twisted together.

The pre-resort town

The early fishing settlement was concentrated around the harbour and to the west of what is today Harbour Street (Fig 5). A little way inland this route was crossed by a path connecting Pegwell Bay to the south-west with the settlements of Hereson, Dumpton and St Peter's to the north-east. The crossroads was known as the Sole, a Kentish term for a pool of standing water and probably a watering place for animals.

Subsequent growth occurred along the four roads converging at the Sole. These were earlier known as West End (renamed High Street about 1800), North End (King Street), South End (Queen Street) and East End (Harbour Street). New streets were laid out extending from the original cruciform structure: the 1717 poor rate assessment records 25 houses at New End, today York Street, of which the Hovelling Boat Inn is an early survivor. To the west was Prince's Court, also known as The Hole on account of a well there, where jettied buildings reportedly survived into the 1880s. By 1635 a brewery and maltings were trading at the end of Queen Street; around 1680 the complex was purchased by Thomas Tomson, whose descendants built up one of the largest brewing businesses in Kent. Amongst the earliest inns and taverns were the King's Head and Royal Oak at the harbour, the Red Lion at the Sole and the Crown Inn at the New End.

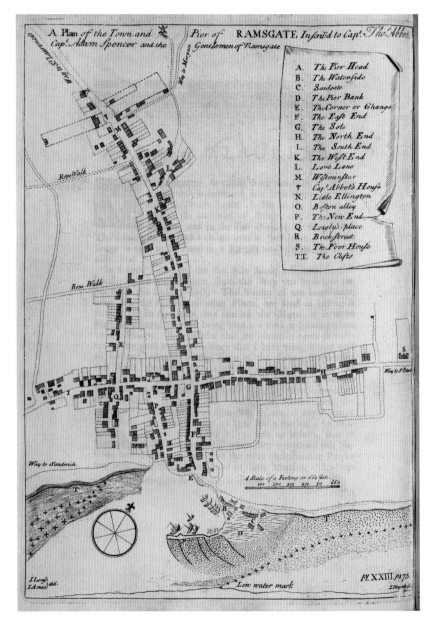

Figure 5
This 1736 map of Ramsgate was prepared for the second edition of John Lewis's history of Thanet. Besides the four principal streets, York Street (The New End) and Effingham Street (Brick Street) are indicated. The two rope walks became George Street and Cannon Road; to the left is a shortcut from the brewery to St Lawrence, part of which survives as Tomson's Passage.
[DP017640, Derek Kendall; © The Society of Antiquaries of London]

Figure 6 (above)
Constructed of neatly coursed and knapped flintwork with brick dressings, 1–2 Queen's Court is a pair of late 17th-century houses, built end-on to Queen Street. It is likely that more buildings of 17th-century date survive behind later facades.
[DP247279]

Figure 7 (above, right)
Chilton Farmhouse was built in the early 18th century for John Curling. Its symmetrical front retains the original wooden mullioned and transomed windows on the first floor, bookended by shaped gables. The present central staircase is a recent addition; the upper floor was originally accessed via winder staircases behind the end stacks.
[DP251255]

Figure 8 (right)
127–135 High Street were probably built in two or more phases in the early 18th century. Set back from the road is No 125, a town house of probable mid-18th-century origin.
[DP247287]

In the last quarter of the 17th century Ramsgate expanded and was rebuilt on the proceeds of coastal trade. In 1673–4, when the town was assessed for the hearth tax, 234 hearths were enumerated in 92 houses while a further 73 houses of the poor were exempt from payment. By that date the town's population was rivalling that of St Lawrence, which had 253 hearths in 100 houses. Houses of any pretension had brick frontages, sometimes reverting to knapped flint at the gable ends. Some were set back behind a front court, like 22 Effingham Street, whose neighbour, No 24, was extended forwards in the later 18th century. Few small houses of late 17th century or early 18th century date survived later rebuilding; a rare example is 15 Harbour Street, a shop and dwelling beneath a steeply pitched roof.

Money could be invested in modernising existing structures or by rebuilding anew (Figs 6–8). In 1723 John Lewis noted that 'the old houses are many of them raised and made very commodious dwellings, and [an] abundance of new ones built after the modern way, in a very elegant and beautiful manner'.[13] Effingham Street first appears on the rate books in 1728 as Brick Street, suggesting that a line of brick houses was then something of a novelty in the town. Piecemeal rebuilding and expansion left a pattern of undeveloped gaps and back plots between building sites. These were occupied by market gardens, nurseries and dairies, the produce from which supplied the town and, via the harbour, the London market.

The harbour

In the early 18th century Ramsgate was in competition with the Cinque Port of Sandwich to be the site of an improved harbour of refuge, the latter proposing a location near Sandown Castle, north of Deal. Minds were focused by the disastrous storm of December 1748 that drove many vessels from their anchorage in the Downs, causing considerable loss of life and shipping. After a petition from ship owners and City of London merchants was considered by a parliamentary committee, an Act of Parliament for enlarging and maintaining Ramsgate harbour received royal assent in 1749, and a board of trustees was constituted.

The design and construction of the new harbour was an expensive and protracted business, fraught with indecision and conflicting advice. After

Figure 9
The inner and outer basins of the harbour are clearly visible in this 2016 aerial photograph, taken from the east. Also prominent is Royal Parade, constructed in the 1890s to improve access to the west cliff.
[29842/034, Damian Grady]

considering various proposals, in January 1750 the trustees opted for two schemes: one by William Ockenden, one of their number, for an east pier of Purbeck stone and another by Captain Robert Brooke for a timber west pier. Thomas Preston was appointed master mason and by July the stone pier was 118m long while the timber pier extended 140m from the west cliff. The ground levels of the foreshore, and what is today Harbour Parade, were built up during its construction so that the floors of older houses ended up below the level of the roadway.

William Etheridge (*c* 1708–76), a master carpenter involved in the construction of Westminster Bridge, was the first resident surveyor and engineer to be appointed, in 1752. In 1754 he erected Jacob's Ladder, a set of wooden stairs that probably ascended to a builders' encampment on the west cliff. The harbour master was directed to hoist a red flag on the signal post at Sion Hill when there was 3m of water at the pier head. In the 19th century this was replaced with a tide ball that was raised and lowered to indicate the tide and which, in rebuilt form, remains in-situ today.

Things took a turn for the worse in December 1753 when the trustees approved Ockenden's proposal to save money by reducing the size of the

RAMSGATE

Figure 10
A view of Ramsgate harbour engraved by Francis
Jukes and first published in 1787. The key includes the
original Jacob's Ladder (marked A), the tide signal (B),
the entrance to the inner basin (C), the custom house (D,
at the King's Head Tavern), the assembly room (E, later
the Albion Hotel), the trustee's office for the works (F)
and the bathing place (G).
[Courtesy of Michael Child]

planned harbour and relocating the west head into deeper water. The ensuing debate brought construction to a halt from 1755–60. As soon as work resumed, another problem became apparent: vast quantities of sand and seaweed were silting up the harbour. Advice was sought from the respected civil engineer John Smeaton (1724–92) who in 1774 proposed an artificial backwater. Pressure created by a head of water collected in an inner basin would be released at low tide from sluice gates, scouring away silt from the harbour. Work on the cross wall, inner basin and sluice gates was completed in 1779 (Fig 9).

The completed harbour became a symbol of Ramsgate's prominence; its piers made the ideal setting for a promenade while crowds gathered to see ships embarking or setting sail (Fig 10). But much remained to be done. A graving or dry dock for the repair of larger vessels, partly influenced by the example at Liverpool Docks, commenced in 1784 and was completed to a revised design in 1791 (Fig 11). In 1788–9 Smeaton devised a diving bell for use in works to extend the east pier. A lighthouse of 1794–5 by his successor, Samuel Wyatt (1737–1807) was one of the first to incorporate a revolving light, powered by a weight that was wound up each day, like a clock.

A Georgian resort

From the early 18th century, taking the sea air, sea bathing, and even drinking sea water were promoted to the social elite as healthy and restorative activities. Margate, Liverpool, Whitby, Scarborough and Brighton were already developing as seasonal resorts by the 1730s, offering bathing facilities, accommodation and respectable places to socialise. Ramsgate was a comparatively late starter: the earliest reference to organised sea bathing dates from May 1754. It takes the form of a small advertisement in the *Kentish Post*:

> At Ramsgate in the Isle of Thanet is lately built a large and convenient machine for the purpose of bathing in the sea. At the same place gentlemen and ladies may be accommodated with very good lodgings, at reasonable rates.[14]

The bathing spot was, of course, Ramsgate Sands, then a more secluded spot than it is today, being sheltered from the town by an outcrop of chalk. The construction of the much-publicised harbour undoubtedly brought a trickle of tourists and is a key feature of early guidebooks. While the odd intrepid bather may have ventured to Ramsgate before the 1750s, it was only at this date that there was sufficient trade to justify the considerable expense of a bathing machine, which conveyed the bather into sufficiently deep water for swimming. It was a cart fitted with a canopy that could be lowered at the rear to allow bathers to enjoy a dip in the sea. The 1759 travel journal of the Mount family, prosperous London stationers, records 'only one bathing machine belonging to Beau Nash'.[15] Richard Nash (1674–1761) was a celebrated dandy and master of ceremonies at the spa towns of Bath and Tunbridge Wells; this intriguing reference to his presence at Ramsgate hints at the connections between Georgian watering places.

The modesty hood attached to the rear of the bathing machine was said to be an invention of the 1750s by Benjamin Beale, a Margate Quaker. Once lowered, this canvas hood, stiffened with hoops, allowed bathers to enter the water and bathe in privacy whilst providing shelter from the wind and waves. Most early versions were intended for one or two bathers, although Charles Dickens's 1836 story 'The Tuggs's at Ramsgate' describes how 'four young ladies,

Figure 11
This plan of the harbour was included in Henry Moses's Picturesque Views of Ramsgate *(1817). Note the newly-completed clock house.*
[Courtesy of Michael Child]

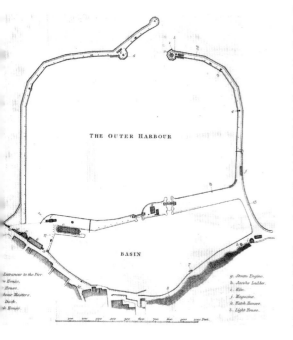

each furnished with a towel, tripped up the steps of a bathing machine'.[16] Local guides (also known as dippers or, confusingly, bathers) provided assistance to those who needed it. There were also more rudimentary waggons with open frames, described by one visitor to Pegwell Bay as 'skeleton machines ... where you are not quite so private as some people would wish to be'.[17]

In 1790, a dozen machines were in use during the summer season, which lasted from June to September. They were owned by a number of competing entrepreneurs: on the arrival of a new operator, John Hope, it was noted that 'the civility and attention shown by his people to the accommodation of the dippers, bid fair to rival, if not eclipse, the same of the other proprietors'.[18] Benjamin West's *The Bathing Place at Ramsgate* (*c* 1788) depicts four machines alongside naked children and female bathers, infants being plunged into the sea by maids and a boy with a crutch partaking of the health-giving waters (Fig 12). The practice of drinking sea water continued well into the 19th century: in 1829 Daniel Benham recorded in his journal that 'Charlotte, myself and the servant each took half a pint of warm salt water'.[19]

James Hawkesley's 'bathing room' in Harbour Street was valued at 3 shillings in the poor rate assessment of August 1764. The provision of this waiting room suggests that the demand for sea bathing had already outstripped the supply of machines by this date, a phenomenon that nearby Margate had begun to address in the same way a decade earlier. Another early bathing entrepreneur was William Cooper, who in 1769 placed a letting advertisement for

> A house, with two very neat waiting rooms for bathing, adjoining ... facing the middle of the harbour, where there is a fine sand and water for bathing. A sober industrious person may have full employ for two machines during the Season. N.B. There will be two Umbrella machines erected, with proper guides to attend them, for accommodating ladies and gentlemen, if the above premises should not be let.[20]

Two bathing rooms are depicted in a drawing of 1781 as weather-boarded huts raised on padstones with curved roofs and small windows; one has a rudimentary porch. An engraving of 1804 shows a twin-celled structure of similar appearance on the site of 100–104 Harbour Parade. The bathing rooms

Figure 12
The Bathing Place at Ramsgate, *of c 1788 by the American painter Benjamin West (1738–1820). Note the bathing machines and bathing room on the pier yard. The stone structure with arched openings is a lime kiln which supplied the construction works at the harbour. [Yale Center for British Art, Paul Mellon Collection]*

opened at around six in the morning and were busiest between seven and nine; names were entered on a slate in the order of their arrival, while newspapers and refreshments were sometimes available. For the Georgian tourist, bathing machines and waiting rooms civilised sea bathing, preserving moral decency and establishing a bathing etiquette that was breached at peril (Fig 13):

> A bathing machine belonging to Hughes was blown down, with two gentlemen in it while bathing [reported the *London Courier and Evening Gazette* in 1801]. The machine was totally demolished and the gentlemen lost a gold watch, and all their clothes—themselves escaping with difficulty. In a state of trepidation and perfect nakedness, they trembled up the steps into the bathing room, where sat some two dozen ladies discussing the essays in a morning paper on the indecency of the bathing at Ramsgate. Only conceive the panic when two naked men presented themselves![21]

Some of Ramsgate's earliest visitors arrived on excursions from Margate or elsewhere in Thanet, while Ramsgate and Broadstairs provided overspill accommodation for those who could not obtain accommodation during high season at Margate. A letter published in August 1768 in the *Kentish Gazette* suggests that Ramsgate was already competing with the longer-established resort at Margate: 'such discoveries and improvements are very lately made at Ramsgate, as will certainly render the bathing place there, equal if not superior, in every desirable respect, to the bay at Margate'.[22] A guide of *c* 1789 drew attention to the contrasting character of the resorts, pronouncing Ramsgate 'more agreeable to those who come more for health than pleasure, being more retired and much less gay and fashionable than [Margate]'.[23] When his correspondent remarked that Margate was livelier than Ramsgate, the poet William Cowper retorted 'so is a Cheshire cheese full of mites more lively than a sound one'.[24]

Scores of guidebooks were aimed at seaside visitors. Sold by local booksellers, often written anonymously, sometimes in the form of a letter to a fictitious friend, they described a resort's features and facilities. One of the earliest guides to feature Ramsgate was *A Description of the Isle of Thanet, and Particularly of the Town of Margate* of 1763. Its author, one 'T G', described the ongoing works at Ramsgate harbour with interest but reckoned the town had 'many good houses, but no great trade'.[25] It is just possible that the author was the poet Thomas Gray, who in February 1767 commended the nascent resort to a convalescing friend: 'It is a neat town, seemingly, with very clean houses to

Figure 13
'A Back-side and Front view of a Modern Fine Lady *vide*
Bunbury or the Swimming Venus of Ramsgate':
Isaac Cruikshank's print of c *1803 satirises the*
fashionable practice of sea bathing.
[© The Trustees of the British Museum]

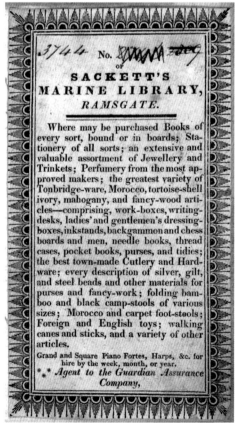

Figure 14 (left)
An early 19th-century sketch of the Albion Hotel and Assembly Rooms, which was opened c 1809 by Henry Bear. The building on the right is part of Goldsmid Place (54–64 Harbour Parade), of 1810 by John Shaw. [DP251293; courtesy of Sally and Rob Holden]

Figure 15 (below, left)
This mid-19th-century photograph shows the bank and circulating library at the corner of High Street and Queen Street. It was built c 1808 for Peter Burgess, who later entered into partnership with W A Hunt. [Courtesy of Phil Spain]

lodge in … it is at no season much pestered with company, and at present, I suppose, there is nobody there'.[26]

Ramsgate's earliest visitors patronised taverns and inns: in 1759 the Mount family 'regailed ourselves at a very handsome publick house commanding the sea'.[27] With the growth of the resort there was sufficient custom to provide the 'company' with accommodation and places of entertainment fitting to their social standing and open to members of both sexes. 'Ramsgate, since the *rage* for sea-bathing hath taken place, has had its share of visitants; and consequently is, every year, much improving in its buildings, and other accommodations', wrote Zechariah Cozens in 1793.[28]

In 1775 Stephen Heritage, the enterprising innkeeper of the King's Head Tavern, opened an assembly room above his coffee house. Here visitors socialised, took refreshments and attended evening balls and 'card parties', the entertainments following a format established by earlier examples at Scarborough, Margate and Hastings, which in turn followed the example of spa towns such as Bath and Tunbridge Wells. Its facilities, provided 'at a very great expense', comprised 'a large and handsome building, consisting of a coffee-room, an elegant public room for ladies and gentlemen to assemble in, withdrawing and other useful rooms (the want of such in the bathing season were generally complained of)'.[29]

Balls were hosted on Tuesday evenings from eight to midnight, while Mondays and Fridays were reserved for games of whist, quadrille, commerce or loo, these activities being regulated by a master of ceremonies. From 1788 the position at both Ramsgate and Margate was held by Charles le Bas, who in 1805 became master of ceremonies at the Lower Rooms in Bath. The King's Head was later eclipsed in reputation by a rival, Henry and Jane Bear's Albion Hotel and Assembly Rooms, which also boasted card rooms and a billiard room. A neat brick building in the Regency style, the hotel hosted popular subscription balls and dinners (Fig 14).

A circulating library was another essential ingredient of the Georgian seaside resort. In August 1776 an enterprising linen draper named Mary Crux diversified by stocking 500 titles at her shop near the King's Head along with 'genteel lodgings'.[30] The bookseller Peter Burgess arrived from Margate around 1786, establishing a library with side lines of toys, stationery and newspapers (Fig 15). Like many proprietors of circulating libraries, he also operated a

Figure 16 (opposite)
Circulating libraries offered more than books, as this bookplate from Sackett's Marine Library advertises. The library was established on Cliff Street by Ann Witherden around 1802, with boarding rooms above. It was taken over by Samuel Sackett in 1819, and remained in business until the 1860s.

printing press, one of several in the town. Its location, opposite the town market, offered 'little prospect, and much smell' according to one guidebook, so that subscribers were provided with 'food for the body and mind at the same time so near at hand'.[31] A smaller library in High Street was run by Ann Witherden, who in the 1800s built a Marine Library at Cliff Street (Fig 16).

Bathhouses allowed delicate or convalescent visitors to bathe in controlled conditions. They were an asset to a seaside resort as they extended the bathing season into the colder months and helped to hedge against the vagaries of the British summer. A warm brine bath was opened in 1790 by a local brazier named Joseph Dyason, following earlier examples at Brighton, Margate, Folkestone and Scarborough. Open from seven in the morning until nine at night, bathers were charged per bath and could choose from four warm baths filled with sea water at each tide, a cold plunge bath and a shower bath. The baths were renamed the Royal Clarence Baths in honour of a royal patron, the Duke of Clarence, later William IV.

By the late 18th century Ramsgate's resort development had outpaced its infrastructure, requiring new forms of investment and renewal. Up to that point, the overseers and surveyor of St Lawrence parish were responsible for the town's upkeep while the town maintained its own poor, building a large poorhouse in 1726 at the present-day junction of Sussex Street and Hardres Street. A vestry meeting of Ramsgate's inhabitants was called in December 1783 to discuss how to better regulate the upkeep of the highways. In 1785 they petitioned Parliament for the power to levy rates to improve the town which, they observed had 'of late years encreased greatly in size and population, and is much resorted to by strangers'.[32]

The resulting Improvement Act empowered the townspeople to levy a local due on coal to clean, light and watch the streets and erect a market house.[33] Sixty commissioners were appointed to fulfil the requirements of the Act, their qualifications for office being possession of land to the value of £25 per annum or a personal estate of £500. Without delay they set about paving the streets in Guernsey and Folkestone stone and resurfacing the foot pavement in flint cobbles. The main sewer, which extended from the Sole to an outfall at the harbour, was rebuilt by the bricklayer Richard Elgar.

Now the town also set about erecting a market house. The commissioner Joseph Stead, a carpenter and surveyor by trade, sold his house, shop and land at the Sole to the commission and in their place erected a timber-framed structure 'of proper scantling'.[34] A subscription room above the market place, plastered and fitted with a Portland stone chimneypiece, was hired out at 10 shillings and sixpence for dancing or concerts. A sail cloth was rigged up over the open-air market below 'to keep the dust and wheather from the market'.[35] The Improvement Act prohibited the sale of any foodstuffs in any other place, except fishermen who could continue to sell fish on the quay and inhabitants who could sell provisions directly from their own property.

The market house provided a balance between commerce, essential to traders and visitors alike, and the propriety expected of a Georgian resort. The commissioners were also empowered to remove 'annoyances' including projecting shop windows, hanging signs, stalls, shelves and lean-to roofs which protruded more than 12 inches (30cm) into the street. Butchers were discouraged from hanging their meat from hooks attached to the lean-to 'penthouses' or pentices; Richard Packer and William Lancefield were prosecuted for 'hanging beasts' heads in the street'.[36] It was forbidden to empty slop pails and pour foul water into the streets and permission was required to dig wells or cesspools. An early instance of street widening in Ramsgate is recorded in 1786 when the commissioner John Farley was compensated for the expense of truncating his property in the narrowest part of Queen Street.

Ramsgate's wealthiest visitors, arriving with their families and an entourage of staff, took a house for several weeks or the entire season. But most visitors rented a suite of rooms in a lodging house, where guests supplied foodstuffs to be cooked by the landlord or landlady, or a boarding house, where board was included. Prices went up in high season, although in 1766 it was reported that provisions at Margate were 20 per cent more expensive than those at Ramsgate, with the result that some Margate bathers travelled to the neighbouring resort 'to dine and sup'.[37]

Although existing dwellings were converted to take paying lodgers, soon they were joined by smart new houses, often incorporating additional rooms or floors to accommodate visitors. In May 1784, two houses belonging to John Boyman and John Mackness were rated 'all for lodgings'.[38] The going rate in 1790 was one guinea per week for a parlour, chamber and the use of a kitchen, although prices rose in July and August when some proprietors insisted on a minimum stay of a month. Inns, while useful stopgap measures for new arrivals, were not generally favoured for long-term stays by genteel visitors. They often required a suite of rooms for several weeks, although rooms were available in the upper floors of the marine library or the assembly rooms.

Effingham Street was a focal point for early lodging houses. Its earliest residences were built for wealthy townspeople but by 1776 it was reckoned 'the most eligible place for persons fond of retirement; it consists of two rows of pretty houses, either let entire, or disposed of for private apartments' for the nobility and gentry.[39] 'Retirement' is probably used here in the archaic sense of a secluded place, but from an early date Ramsgate was favoured by sea captains, ship owners, military men and their widows as a place of retirement in the contemporary sense. Paradise, first rated in 1779, was said to be popular with sailors in their dotage.

As demand for accommodation grew, so operations were scaled up with the erection of whole terraces. These were purchased to live in, to operate as a lodging house, or some combination of the two. John Fagg (1728–95), a Ramsgate attorney, was amongst the first to introduce this form of property speculation to the town. Realising that a considerable profit was to be made in buying fields on the fringe of the town and selling them on as building land, in 1768 he advertised two acres of arable on the west cliff as 'well situated for building on, and commanding a very fine and extensive prospect on both sea and land'.[40] This is an early reference to the monetisation of Ramsgate's sea views, a decisive factor in the town's development.

Ramsgate's first unified terrace was Chapel Place, built c 1788–90 by John Horn on land owned by Fagg (Fig 17). Respectability and prestige were conferred by a central chapel of ease, dedicated to St Mary, which saved worshippers the uphill journey to St Laurence. This plain, portico'd place of worship was funded by Fagg, Horn, the Revd Richard Harvey, the vicar of St Laurence and others, and consecrated in 1791 by the Archbishop of Canterbury. The houses have wide plots but a glance at the backs shows that only the front portion rises to the full three storeys, with lower wings at the rear. The south side of the street was not developed, leaving uninterrupted sea views; when Fagg conveyed houses there to James Townley, he undertook to 'not shut out the view of the sea'.[41] It was later laid out with pleasure gardens by Townley's son, Robert.

Figure 17
Chapel Place, of c 1788–90, is Ramsgate's earliest speculative terrace.
[DP251309]

As the town became busier and more commercial in character, the cornfields on the cliffs were eyed up as potential locations for high-class accommodation. Lady Mary Coke recorded in her 1788 journal, 'I've got a new built house upon the cliff from hence I see nothing – but the sea – this is better than being in a dirty town'.[42] As Chapel Place neared completion, work started on Albion Place, the first major development on the east cliff. Its L-shaped layout of two adjacent terraces ignored the existing street pattern, instead looking out over the harbour and the open sea. At the centre was a landscaped pleasure garden in the form of a lawn enclosed by iron railings and fitted out with benches. It was as if a London square had been set down and sliced open to reveal the sea view (Fig 18).

Albion Place provides an insight into the dynamics of resort development. Its name appealed to a growing sense of national identity, reinforced by apprehension of the Irish Rebellion and the upheavals in France. In 1789 the innkeeper Stephen Heritage bought a prominent site on the east cliff, devised a layout and sold off most of the 28 plots directly to individual purchasers, who in turn had houses built to their own specifications. Four plots, for example, were purchased by James Townley who by 1792 had erected Nos 12–16. Like many developers, Heritage retained a degree of control on subsequent construction by tying to each transaction a 'deed of stipulations and restrictions' which specified when and how the houses were to be built. Such covenants were often used to impose visual uniformity on the facades; where they were absent or unenforced the result was a terrace of haphazard appearance, with visible variations in building height, layout and detailing.

Four pairs of plots were purchased in 1791 by the carpenter Stephen Peake, the bricklayer Thomas Woodland and Thomas Grey, a baker who may have fronted the working capital. Construction was financed by selling off the properties in advance (sometimes known as 'off plan' today). Albion House, the prestigious townhouse at the seaward end, is a case in point. In 1791 they sold a pair of plots to James Simmons (1741–1807). A prominent Canterbury alderman, Simmons in 1768 founded his own newspaper, the *Kentish Gazette,* and between 1790 and 1803 landscaped the Dane John Gardens in that city. Albion House was probably completed in 1794, the year it first appears on the rate books. From the outset it was rented out as a furnished lodging house, being let to the Archbishop of Canterbury in 1810 and Princess Victoria in 1835.

Figure 18
Albion Place was the first terrace development to be completed on the seafront. It was a popular location for lodging houses.
[DP251338]

Drawn & Eng.d by W.Deeble.

East Cliff Lodge, Thanet.

Figure 19
East Cliff Lodge was built for Benjamin Bond Hopkins
MP but subsequently passed into the hands of numerous
owners including Admiral Viscount Keith and Sir Moses
Montefiore.
[DP251319; courtesy of Sally and Rob Holden]

By 1776 Lord Conyngham and Earl Verney possessed townhouses for use in the summer season. Of somewhat different character were the landed 'marine villas' which from the 1790s appeared along the seafront at a remove from the town. They were occasionally made available to members of the royal family or aristocracy for the season, confirming their elite status. East Cliff Lodge was built in the Tudor Gothic style by the Margate surveyor Charles Boncey for Benjamin Bond Hopkins MP (Fig 19). Unfinished at the time of Hopkins's death in 1794, it subsequently passed through the hands of a succession of owners. In the summer of 1803 it was rented to Caroline of Brunswick, Princess of Wales, where it was alleged that she conducted an affair with a naval officer. At about the same time Joseph Ruse commissioned Belmont, a marine villa with Gothick trimmings on the west cliff. In 1836 it hosted Princess Victoria who described it as 'small, & anything but cheerful'.[43]

The fashion for sea bathing had wider impacts on the resort's hinterland. A 1763 guidebook to Thanet predicted that the 'late great resort of gentry to this place' would soon push up the price of local farm produce, while noting that local landowners had erected signposts and straightened the local tracks to avoid 'having their corn trampled down' by tourist carriages.[44] Many of Ramsgate's earliest visitors arrived in their own coaches, stabling at the Bull and George Inn or the London Hotel, which opened in 1789 on the corner of High Street and King Street. For those who could afford it, a stagecoach ran between London and Ramsgate, a journey of two days and one night. With the introduction of the safety coach the journey could be made in a single day. Access to Ramsgate was further opened up with the construction of turnpike roads from Ramsgate to Canterbury via Sarre, achieved through an 1802 Act of Parliament and, following an Act of 1807, connecting the town with Sandwich and Margate. A tollhouse serving the former was located on the site of the present Nethercourt roundabout.

Why did Margate's resort story start so much earlier than did Ramsgate's? Part of the answer is to do with its accessibility from London by river. Due to its sheltered location on the mouth of the Thames Estuary, Margate was served by a regular and inexpensive passenger service from the capital at an early date. To arrive at Ramsgate it was necessary to skirt the North Foreland, braving the choppy waters of the open sea. The sea passage was especially risky in times of war: in August 1760 the *Derby Mercury* reported the sorry plight of eight London tradesmen who chartered a vessel to Ramsgate on a 'party of pleasure' but who were hijacked by French privateers at the North Foreland.[45]

The first regular service from London to the Thanet resorts was made by hoys or packets, built as cargo vessels and converted for passenger use. In 1779 William Cowper observed that 'the hoy went to London every week, loaded with mackerel and herrings, and returned loaded with company. The cheapness of the conveyance made it equally commodious for dead fish and lively company'.[46] During the summer season, hoys sailed twice a week to Ramsgate from Botolph Wharf near London Bridge, sailing time varying according to tides and weather. Other visitors preferred to avoid weathering the North Foreland by taking a hoy to Margate and completing the journey by stagecoach. According to one 1765 account, 'the hoy, like the grave, confounds all distinctions: high and low, rich and poor, sick and sound, are here indiscriminately blended together', while 18th century cartoonists relished the satirical possibilities offered by a queasy combination of social contrasts, drunkenness and seasickness.[47] Later, different classes of accommodation were introduced with fares priced accordingly.

'Who would not, dear mother, to Ramsgate repair,
To gain health from the ocean and flirt with the fair?'

'Simkin Slenderwit', *The Sea-Side, a Poem*, 1798[48]

Ramsgate before the railway

3   Ramsgate in the Napoleonic Wars

In the 1790s, against the background of the French Revolution and concern over riots and radicalism at home, Ramsgate turned from the business of pleasure to that of war. Thanet was relatively lightly protected during the Napoleonic Wars in comparison with the areas around Chatham and Dover; the focus of the east Kent defences was Deal, which was equipped with a barracks, naval yard and castle. But Ramsgate's recently completed harbour was of national importance as a port of embarkation for troops, horses and supplies (Fig 20). Military Road was built along the landward side of the inner harbour *c* 1808 in anticipation of large-scale embarkations. Large elements of the force sent to face down Napoleon in 1815 left via the harbour, including cavalry and artillery. In 1803 the Royal Engineers installed a total of five gun batteries, two on the east cliff and three on the west cliff, for the defence of the harbour and the protection of the fishing fleet against French privateers.

In May 1794 a general meeting was held at Ramsgate for the defence of the Cinque Ports, resulting in the formation of three companies of the Ramsgate Volunteer Infantry. Another militia corps was the Sea Fencibles, a voluntary force of mariners established to defend the coast in the event of a French landing. In 1803–4, the Ramsgate District was briefly commanded by (Sir) Francis William Austen, the brother of Jane Austen and later admiral of the fleet. The coexistence of the volunteer units and the regular regiments stationed at the barracks was at times uneasy: when, in 1804, at the height of the invasion scare, a detachment of the 1st Surrey Militia was called out to a house fire, it was reported that 'the Sea Fencibles, and boatmen of every description, were on the alert, in full expectation that the French had landed'.[49]

In 1799 the West Yorkshire Militia were stationed at a 'barracks at the back of Albion Place', but by the following year an army base had been established on the west cliff in the area of the present-day Spencer Square.[50] 'Barracks' conjures up an image of a defensible compound, complete with stoutly built

Military Road and the west cliff as it appeared before its reconstruction in the 1890s. Just about visible on the west cliff is Sion Hill, the Foy Boat Tavern and the harbour signal. This is the left-hand image of a pair of stereo photographs taken by John C Twyman, who was active as a Ramsgate photographer from the 1860s. In stereoscopic photography two slightly offset photographs, when viewed through a stereoscope, create the illusion of a three dimensional image. [DP251296; courtesy of Sally and Rob Holden]

Figure 20
Embarking Troops and Horses at Ramsgate: *a watercolour of c 1800 by John Augustus Atkinson. [© National Maritime Museum, Greenwich, London]*

accommodation blocks, officers' quarters, a mess house and stables. But Ramsgate's Napoleonic barracks was a temporary base, intended to operate for the duration of the war and no longer. It combined the functions of transit camp, rendezvous point and supply depot for regiments awaiting embarkation or for those returning from duty overseas pending marching orders. In July 1805, 829 infantry and 169 cavalry with 161 horses were stationed at Ramsgate, with 40 patients in an improvised hospital.

It is likely that the Board of Ordnance came to an arrangement to rent land and buildings from the Townley family, one of the town's principal landholders. James Townley is first recorded as the freehold owner of barrack accommodation in the poor rate assessment of February 1800. Between 1798 and 1804 he assembled the land on which his wife Mary Townley designed 35–42 Spencer Square (originally 1–8 Spencer Place) and the adjacent 1–3 Royal Road (Fig 21). It is said that these houses first served as officers' quarters, and whether or not this is the case their layout is quite different to the speculative terraces going up elsewhere at Ramsgate. A series of small back yards separates the terrace from a rear range; they are spanned at first-floor level by a linking passage with a wc. The rear rooms may have accommodated the officer's orderlies. Each house was lit by only a single window per floor, whereas most comparable terraced houses were three bays wide. In front of Spencer Place was an enclosed parade ground and exercise yard, while a detached building to the north-east may have been the residence of the commanding officer (Fig 22).

To the north, on Spencer Mews (present-day Townley Street), James Townley laid out ranges of stables and a coach house, enclosed by brick walls and entered from Addington Street. Next to the gateway was a terrace of three small houses, possibly used by stable orderlies. Nearby was a 'new house' rated in 1808 at eight shillings to the barrack-master William Braybrooke.[51] It was customary for the soldiers to be accompanied by their families; an 1809 inspection found that the barracks were occupied by 'the whole of the women and children of the 50th regiment', adding that women were 'a great nuisance in these barracks'.[52]

Numbers stationed at Ramsgate fluctuated according to wider patterns of troop movements. Soldiers unable to be accommodated at the barracks may have encamped during the summer or been quartered in private houses: three of James Townley's houses in Chapel Place served as billets in February 1812 as did

Figure 21 (right)
The earliest surviving elements of Spencer Square are Nos 35–42. This terrace of eight white-rendered houses was built in the early 1800s by the Townley family and initially formed part of the barracks accommodation.
[DP247250]

Figure 22
An extract from Collard and Hurst's 1822 map of Ramsgate, showing the site of the former barracks in present-day Spencer Square. The long structure to the north of Spencer Place was the associated stables and coach houses, while the nearby Duke of York pub is said to have originated as a soldiers' canteen.
[Courtesy of Michael Child]

a property of his in Chatham Street in April 1815. The arrival in 1809 of large numbers of sick troops from the Walcheren campaign prompted criticism of the insanitary and inadequate accommodation at the barracks. After an inspection it was recommended that the mess rooms and other spaces were converted temporarily into hospital wards.

The military presence had a far-reaching social and economic impact on the town and resort. Large-scale embarkations were dramatic events which drew large numbers of spectators. Fraternisation between soldiers and the civilian population took place at all social levels, from ballroom to brothel. The war affected Ramsgate families in unexpected ways: in 1809 James and Mary Townley married off their daughter Caroline to Lieutenant Rudolph Pringle of the King's German Legion. The following year their youngest son, Lieutenant Poyntz Stepney Townley, was killed during an attack on a French convoy off the Île de Ré. Ramsgate was popular as a seasonal base or a place of retirement with naval men such as Admiral Viscount Keith (1746–1823), commander of the Channel fleet, who purchased East Cliff Lodge as a marine villa around 1804. Despite the military presence and the threat of invasion, the growth of the seaside resort continued largely unabated, due in part to the visits of officers' friends and family and the presence of wealthy visitors unable to holiday on the Continent.

The provision of food, drink and equipment was a further stimulus to local trade. Addington Street sprang up in the 1800s to provide stores and taverns (Fig 23). A soldiers' canteen was rated at 12 shillings to John Ansell in 1810; it is said to have been located at No 25, later the Duke of York pub. A painted coat of arms at the Queen Charlotte pub may also commemorate the Napoleonic period. With loyalism came local benefits: when in 1797 Mary Townley presented a pair of regimental colours to the Ramsgate volunteers, she tellingly expressed the hope that they would be employed for 'purposes connected with the general defence of our country, and with the prosperity of Ramsgate in particular'.[53]

After victory at Waterloo troops returned via Ramsgate harbour. But as soon as December 1815 the *Kentish Weekly Post* reported 'the Ramsgate Barracks have been given up, which seems not a little extraordinary at this time, when troops may be expected to arrive here daily from Ostend'.[54] Spencer Place was converted to private residences and lodging houses (the houses were recorded as 'preparing' in an 1818 rate book entry), although the rest of Spencer Square and Royal Road was not laid out until the mid-1830s.[55]

Figure 23
A view down Addington Street towards the seafront.
The weatherboarded No 41 was erected between 1806
and 1817 by the cordwainer Abraham Staples.
[DP247189]

Getting there

At the end of the Napoleonic War, coal-fired steam boats first appeared at Margate. Larger, cheaper and more dogged in poor weather than sailing packets, they brought tourists in ever-increasing numbers. The *Thames* (popularly known as the *Margery*), a steam packet with a single 14-horsepower engine, plied between London and Margate from 1815. The Ramsgate mariner and sometime harbour master Kennett Beacham Martin (1788–1859), then captaining a sailing packet, described his first encounter with the steamer: 'I believe it was in June 1815, that, on my passage from Ramsgate to London, my companions, with great alarm, pointed out to me an object at some distance in our head-way, which they supposed to be a vessel on fire'. Despite its slow speed, clumsy appearance and halo of smoke, he perceived in the *Thames* 'the future triumph of steam in short voyages'.[56]

It was joined in 1816 by the 25-hp *Majestic*, built by the Ramsgate shipwright William Caught, while the *Sons of Commerce* of 1817 hinted at the sizable profits to be made by such ventures.[57] In 1821 Martin was asked to captain the first steam packet to serve Ramsgate. The *Eagle* set off from the Custom House stairs near London Bridge every Wednesday and Saturday morning, returning on Mondays and Thursdays.[58] With the introduction of faster steamers in the mid-19th century workers were able to join their families on the Saturday evening 'husbands' boat' or 'hat boat' from London.[59] Smoother and better appointed, the steamers afforded the opportunity to relax and socialise. In August 1820 the architect William Porden recounted a return journey in the *London Engineer* steam yacht:

We glided along as quietly as if we had been sitting in a drawing [room]. In
the handsome and spacious cabin, some were playing at cards, some at
chess, some at draughts or backgammon and some reading. On the deck we
had the same amusements, and music, solos on the harp etc and after
dinner dancing for three or four hours.[60]

As the steamboat service became cheaper and more reliable, access to the resort
was widened to those who had hitherto been unable to afford it, diversifying and
commercialising Ramsgate's growing seaside economy. In a highly stratified
society all modes of public transport were to some extent places of social mixing
(or 'mixed company', to use a contemporary phrase). How one arrived at a resort
attracted the attentions of social commentators and snobs: 'at Margate we saw

plenty of "hoy" people dressed in buff slippers or shoes, nankeen unspeakables & duffy coats or dressing gowns', one visitor recorded in a 1828 travel journal. Of Ramsgate he noted 'I believe since the steamers have frequented it the company has very much fallen off'.[61]

'The entertainment of visitors or felicity hunters'[62]

Those arriving at Ramsgate harbour in the early 19th century were confronted with quite a welcome party. The soundscape must have been remarkable: the bustle of disembarking passengers mixing with lodging house touts and the drivers of fly carriages (a light, horse-drawn coach). Crowds thronged to the

Figure 24
This watercolour of the harbour from the east cliff was painted in 1802 by J R Smith junior. The recently completed lighthouse, pier house and harbour master's house stand out against the older, brick-and-tile houses of the town. The barrel vaulted structure opposite the harbour gates is a bathers' waiting room. Note also the steps descending to the harbour (later rebuilt as Kent Steps), the original Jacob's Ladder and Sion Hill and Prospect Terrace on the west cliff.
[Guy Peppiatt Fine Art]

harbour to watch the boats come and go, while beggars, itinerant musicians and the cries of food vendors (selling muffins, mackerel, eels, shrimps and cakes) loom large in contemporary accounts of Ramsgate street life.

Increasing demand justified further investment in the bathing facilities. By 1815, 20 bathing machines were available: those reserved for ladies operated nearest the pier, with the gentlemen's machines a respectable distance away. The waiting rooms on the site of 100–104 Harbour Parade were extended or rebuilt after the removal of a section of the chalk promontory (Fig 24). They were joined by Pier Castle (94–98 Harbour Parade), probably completed in 1818 as rented accommodation for bathing machine proprietors and their employees (Fig 25). Its turreted and crenelated silhouette was not long completed when it was sketched by J M W Turner.

After bathing, it was common to stroll on the pier and take breakfast. As early as 1829 chairs could be hired at the beach to enjoy the view while maintaining a relatively formal posture and avoid sitting in the soft sand. Sea shells and flints were collected (the latter for the tinder box) and sandcastles erected. Donkey rides on the beach were available from the early 19th century, and a visitor in 1823 noticed Princess Victoria engaged in this pursuit, attended by two grooms and ladies in waiting. Pleasure trips out of the harbour were another popular pursuit. In 1759 the Mount family chartered a fishing vessel at the harbour, sailing as far as Deal. Soon, small boats could be hired by the hour together with a skipper. By 1828 a *camera obscura* was installed on the west pier. This was a small structure with a periscope protruding above its roof which projected images of the sea and harbour onto a white table inside.

Visitors were curious about the working life of the resort, inspecting the harbour structures and vessels moored there but also venturing further afield. It was common to make afternoon drives to Pegwell Bay, Margate, Broadstairs and private estates accessible to visitors such as Dandelion near Margate and Lord Holland's house at Kingsgate. An annual Ramsgate regatta was held from 1834 under the patronage of Sir William Curtis (1752–1829), chairman of the harbour trustees. It included races between the luggers and galleys of Ramsgate and neighbouring ports and concluded with a contest between 'the oldest worn-out boatmen belonging to the town, with prizes of beef, mutton, port, tea and tobacco'.[63]

In June 1816, the luxurious Isabella Baths (later renamed the Royal Kent Baths) opened at the end of the recently completed Paragon terrace (Fig 26). Designed by Robert Stuart Meikleham on the model of the warm baths at Naples, the single-storey structure contained a central, bow-fronted saloon which boasted fine views and daily newspapers. Flanking doors gave access to male and female wings, each containing six top-lit baths. Steam generated by boilers was conveyed through underfloor pipes into a vase placed in a central niche in each bathing compartment, while sea water was pumped up through the cliff with a steam engine. The bathing cubicles were clad in white marble,

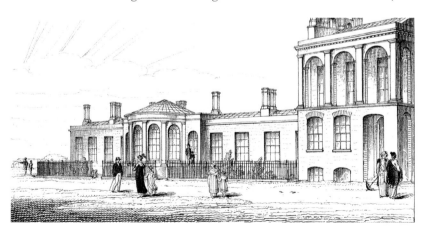

Figure 26
An illustration of the Isabella Baths appears in Henry Moses's Picturesque Views of Ramsgate *(1817). The adjoining house (16 Paragon) may have accommodated the proprietor.*
[Courtesy of Michael Child]

giving them 'quite the air of an ancient Roman bath'.[64] Messrs Foat and Barling's waiting rooms were in 1836 redeveloped as the Victoria Baths. An early project by the Ramsgate architect and surveyor George Martin Hinds (1804–80), the complex included shops, reading rooms and six private baths, each with a shower and dressing room, all housed behind an Ionic colonnade.

Although recitals were sometimes given at the libraries, Ramsgate lacked a concert hall or theatre and so formal recitals tended to be semi-private affairs for subscribers. The 'fashionable lounge' held in 1802 at Signora Morelle's on Sion Hill included a grand pedal harp accompanying an 'uncommonly fine counter-tenor voice'.[65] About 1813 William Goldfinch opened a recital room at the newly developed Hardres Street. An elaborate building with a domed roof and weathervane, it was popularly known as the Cock and Fiddle. Musicians could also be procured for more private moments: in 1788, Lady Mary Coke 'gave some money to a French horn and an organ to play me to sleep'.[66]

Ramsgate's tradition of seaside bands, which played such a prominent part in its 19th-century soundscape, may originate in the regiments and voluntary militias of the Napoleonic Wars. Military bands brought new and unfamiliar instruments and repertoires: in 1807 it was reported that 'the departure of the fine band of the [King's German Legion] is viewed with the utmost regret, by all our fashionables, as they have tended much to enliven the evening promenades, on the crescent, the pier, and at the public libraries'.[67]

More prevalent was amateur music-making. By 1810 the Apollo Catch Club was active in Ramsgate, meeting at various inns. This was a male-only musical club for the singing of catches or canons, and seems to have been frequented by residents rather than visitors. The latter entertained themselves in the evening by playing cards or making music on portable instruments or the pianos provided at some lodging houses and public venues. One mid-19th-century account describes how evenings were passed

> on the terraces [by] groups of lazy promenaders, balcony parties, flirting and laughing with each other; and musical parties, from which the sounds of the piano and the harp float through the open windows into the cool night-air.[68]

Figure 27
St James's Hall on Broad Street. This entertainment
venue of 1861 stands on the site of Ramsgate's earliest
purpose-built theatre, opened in 1825 by Faucet Saville.
[DP24271]

Unlike Margate, whose Theatre Royal opened in 1787, Ramsgate lacked a performing arts venue, due in part to the difficulty of obtaining a licence from the Lord Chamberlain. A short-lived theatre was opened in 1825 in Broad Street by Faucet Saville, the proprietor of Margate's theatre. Built by Thomas Areton Grundy, James Craven and Elvy John Wildish with the financial support of Sir William Curtis, it featured a painted curtain and tiers of boxes in salmon and gold, decorated with roses, thistles and shamrocks. After a disastrous fire in 1829, the venue was rebuilt in 1831 and over subsequent decades successively functioned as a temperance hall, theatre, chapel and auction house (Fig 27). Its chequered fate demonstrates that running a theatre was a risky enterprise, subject to fires, censorship and the changing whims of the paying public.

Staying there: lodging houses

Some visitors pre-booked accommodation by prior arrangement with the proprietor or a friend. Regular visitors often returned to their favoured lodgings; in 1829 Daniel Benham describes how he 'found our old lodgings engaged therefore took a sitting room and two bedrooms at Mr Cullen's in Hertford Place'.[69] Others found a place on the spot, looking out for notices in the windows of houses which were available to let. In 'The Tuggs's at Ramsgate', Dickens describes a middling family's quest for affordable lodgings:

> It had grown dusk when the 'fly' – the rate of whose progress greatly belied its name – after climbing up four or five perpendicular hills, stopped before the door of a dusty house, with a bay window, from which you could obtain a beautiful glimpse of the sea – if you thrust half of your body out of it, at the imminent peril of falling into the area. Mrs Tuggs alighted. One ground-floor sitting-room, and three cells with beds in them up-stairs. A double-house. Family on the opposite side. Five children milk-and-watering in the parlour, and one little boy, expelled for bad behaviour, screaming on his back in the passage.[70]

Speculative terraced houses boasted sufficiently flexible layouts to accommodate residents, to provide lodgings or some combination of the two. Dickens seems to describe a double-fronted house, with the owner on one side of a central hallway and the guests on the other. But such layouts were then relatively uncommon in Ramsgate, when most middle-class visitors would take the entire floor of a terraced house. Most of the terraces had front and back rooms heated by stacks on one party wall and a dog-leg stair against the other. Referring to the uniformity of this arrangement, one visitor observed that 'the lodging houses are so numerous as to form whole streets or rows, and they are all constructed entirely upon the London plan'.[71] The double-fronted houses in Chapel Place sport the more unusual layout of lateral stacks with stairs pushed back to the rear of the central bay.

In streets perpendicular to the seafront, bay windows of bowed or canted form were essential to a proprietor's claim of a sea view, as well as being suitable forms for shop windows. In 1822 the poet Samuel Taylor Coleridge stayed at the end house in Plains of Waterloo, 'having a certain modicum and segment of sea-peep'.[72] In theory such projections were regulated by the town's improvement commissioners and could be the cause of dispute. A legal agreement of 1841 noted that a neighbour's bay window 'interferes with my own sea view'.[73] A first-floor balcony with a veranda became a standard ingredient of the seafront terrace, and these were sometimes ingeniously combined with bow windows, as at the elegant early Victorian terraces on Augusta Road.

Always more numerous in Ramsgate than hotels, boarding houses developed their own protocol. Breakfast, lunch and dinner were provided, and according to one late 19th-century source a communal atmosphere prevailed at some houses: 'at the last-named meal there is usually a president elected for the week, whose word is held to be law. Old habitués of these boarding-houses have their seats at table reserved for them from season to season'.[74] Many lodging house keepers were female, as this was considered a respectable occupation and one which could be combined with child care or provide a source of income for widows.

Speculative building

The pioneering developments of Chapel Place and Albion Place were followed by several smaller groups of lodging houses raised in the 1790s along the seafront of the west cliff, including Sion Hill, Prospect Place and Prospect Hill. The

Figure 28
Nelson Crescent was gradually built up over about a
decade from 1799. Its varied appearance suggests that
individual plots or pairs of plots were separately
developed.
[DP247184]

Napoleonic Wars did nothing to abate speculation; if anything the local presence of the military barracks stimulated more extensive terraces on the west cliff for officers' families, bearing the suitably patriotic names of Trafalgar Place and Nelson Crescent (*c* 1799–1809; Fig 28). The former, at 37–67 West Cliff Road, was developed from *c* 1807 by the carpenter Daniel Bayly Jarman and others and is today much altered. Paragon (completed 1818), aside from alluding to The Paragon in Bath, may commemorate a transport ship of that name which conveyed troops from the harbour. The topical naming of Wellington Crescent and the adjacent Plains of Waterloo (1818–24) after the Duke of Wellington's 1815 victory against Napoleon recalls the passage in Jane Austen's unfinished novel *Sanditon* (1817) in which the seaside landholder Mr Parker ponders the names of his building ventures:

> You will not think I have made a bad exchange when we reach Trafalgar
> House – which by the bye, I almost wish I had not named Trafalgar – for
> Waterloo is more the thing now. However Waterloo is in reserve; & if we
> have encouragement enough this year for a little crescent to be ventured on

(as I trust we shall) then we shall be able to call it Waterloo Crescent – and the name joined to the form of the building, which always takes, will give us the command of lodgers.[75]

Most seafront terraces looked out onto a communal garden, which provided a prestigious feature while ensuring the preservation of sea views. These valuable amenities could be safeguarded by writing covenants into property deeds which prohibited the erection of any structures on gardens or forward of a defined building line. When Stephen Heritage sold plots on Albion Place in 1791 he retained possession of the garden, undertaking not to prejudice 'the prospect from the houses to be erected'.[76] Unusually, the 1820s terrace originally known as Adelaide Place (25–32 Adelaide Gardens) was provided with long private gardens at the front. Covenants of Ramsgate properties could also prohibit building work during the summer season, regarded then as now as a nuisance to holidaymakers. When in 1837 Mary Townley sold the future site of Kent Place she prohibited construction works between 1 July and 1 November and any houses higher than the parapet wall at the top of the cliff, safeguarding views from Albion Place.

Figure 29
Although Wellington Crescent was completed piecemeal over several years, architectural unity is achieved through the continuous colonnade, veranda and the stepping up in height towards the centre.
[DP251318]

Who designed Ramsgate's Georgian and Regency set-pieces? It might be argued that the modern conception of a professional architect – one who supplies drawings and oversees construction – only arrived in Ramsgate with A W N Pugin (page 82), although Mary Townley represents a notable precursor. There is little evidence in early 19th-century Ramsgate for any hard-and-fast division of labour between design, building and related activities such as surveying and valuing. In most cases, layouts and details were determined by the building contractor, perhaps with reference to pattern books or fashionable examples in London, Bath or Brighton. Most builders entered the trade as carpenters or bricklayers, and one 18th-century commentator observed that 'a master-bricklayer thinks himself capable to raise a brick-house without the tuition of an architect'.[77]

Speculative builders came in many forms. Initiated in a booming local economy, Wellington Crescent and Plains of Waterloo on the east cliff were the joint venture of four local tradesmen: the blacksmith James Underdown, the shipwright William Miller, the builder James Smith and the carpenter Pilcher Longley. Like many small-time speculative builders, they used their limited working capital to erect a number of brick shells or 'carcasses'. These they sold off with the option to fit out the interiors for an additional sum. Other plots were sold on to others to develop. The elevations rise in height towards the centre, from three storeys to four to taller four-storeyed houses, avoiding monotony while providing three different specifications. Unity is imposed by a continuous Doric colonnade and first-floor veranda (Fig 29). In 1825 the newly completed crescent hosted the Duke of Wellington himself.

Taking on a development on this scale was fraught with risk as well as opportunity. Smith, a bricklayer by trade, worked extensively on the east cliff where he established a builder's yard on King Street and around 1818 erected Waterloo Cottage (50 Plains of Waterloo) for his family. His son, William Edward Smith (1816–89), became a successful Victorian master builder, alternating between the roles of architect and contractor. Miller owned the gardens in front of Wellington Crescent, where in 1825 he put up an oak statue of Wellington. He lived at Albion Place nearby but in 1844 commissioned G M Hinds to design East Cliff House, a detached house beside Wellington Crescent. Longley and Underdown, on the other hand, were declared bankrupt in the 1820s and their real estate was liquidated to pay off their debts.

Most new terraces and streets were named after royals or nobles. The

central pediment of Liverpool Lawn (*c* 1827–36) bears the arms of the Earl of Liverpool, Lord Warden of the Cinque Ports and long-serving prime minster. These elegant Regency terraces were put up by the Ramsgate builder-developers James Crisford and D B Jarman (Fig 30). Royal Kent Terrace (1833–7) was one of several resort developments which commemorate the Duchess of Kent, the

Figure 30
Liverpool Lawn was planned as a gently curving crescent to exploit sea views from its site, which is set back from the seafront. Note the curved sashes and header bond of the sea-facing, bow-fronted return elevation.
[DP251331]

mother of Princess Victoria and a regular visitor to Ramsgate. This L-shaped terrace, a miniature version of nearby Albion Place, was formed by cutting back the rocky chalk escarpment. Directly accessible from the beach, the row stands proudly at the centre of William Frith's *Ramsgate Sands*.

Mary Townley, a Ramsgate architect

Access to capital was easier for James and Mary Townley who speculated in land and property on an even larger scale. James Townley (1745–1817) was a successful proctor or attorney, practicing at Doctors' Commons in London and having professional interests in Canterbury. He started to invest his disposable income in Ramsgate property in the early 1780s, assembling a considerable portfolio of land on the west cliff and elsewhere. At first the couple resided in Clapham, but it is clear that they became attached to Ramsgate and gradually established themselves there. Townley held several lodging houses which generated a rental income, elsewhere selling on building land for a profit. On the occasions that he built, the designs were often supplied by his wife.

In the figure of Mary Townley (1754–1839) we not only have one of the first instances of an architect operating in Ramsgate, but one of the earliest women architects recorded anywhere (Fig 31). Although married women were not legally entitled to own landed property in their own right, the evidence suggests that she operated with relative autonomy in her family's property dealings, bidding at auctions and negotiating land deals. Mary continued these activities after the death of her husband, sometimes cooperating with her son Robert on developments. She continued to derive an income from rental property, and in 1833 willed the considerable sum of £5 to Jane Tunbridge 'who has the care of my lodging houses in Albion Place'.[78]

A skilled and imaginative designer, Mary was well versed in domestic classicism, with a penchant for the picturesque 'Gothick' style. She was said to be an accomplished artist who learned to paint by copying portraits by Sir Joshua Reynolds who was known to her husband's family. It is likely that she directed building operations too. In 1810 she took out a patent for 'the prevention or cure of smokey chimnies', suggesting practical experience of how buildings were put together and serviced.[79]

Figure 31
A portrait of Mary Townley in later life, painted by Henry Room (1802–50).
[DP251328; courtesy of John Farley]

Figure 32
Townley House was built in 1792 by James and Mary Townley on land purchased in 1789 from Mary Garrett of Ellington. It was the holiday residence of the Duchess of Kent and Princess Victoria in 1822, 1823, 1824 and 1827.
[DP247259]

Figure 33
This postcard of Townley Castle dates from the First World War, when it was used as a military hospital for Canadian soldiers.
[Courtesy of Ralph Hoult]

Townley House, the family's townhouse on Chatham Street, was completed in 1792. Broad and white rendered, it features a great central bow, raised on Tuscan columns to form an entrance portico (Fig 32). Its large reception rooms were the location for society balls and masquerades, and the house was given over to the Duchess of Kent and Princess Victoria on several occasions in the 1820s. Entertaining guests was evidently a priority for the Townleys, who by 1809 had built Townley Castle, a guests' annexe in its own grounds (Fig 33). It was an idiosyncratic, folly-like structure of rendered brick with lancet windows and battlements. Those demolishing the building in the 1920s discovered multiple floor levels, inscriptions and curios such as a column in the form of a lighthouse which concealed a miniature spiral staircase.

Most of the buildings developed by the Townleys were probably intended to be rented out or sold on, including 35–42 Spencer Square and 1–3 Royal Road (c 1802–5), Pier Castle (c 1818), Royal Crescent (from 1826) and Devonshire Place (23–24 Paragon, of c 1830). It is probable that Mary Townley also built 12–16 Albion Place, although its design was regulated by a deed of stipulations. Royal Crescent, overseen by Mary's son Robert, was the family's largest single scheme on their extensive estate west of Royal Road. It was originally intended to be twice its present length, at 292m and yielding 38 houses. But despite the prestigious seafront site only eight houses had been erected by 1839 and its palace front, with its distinctive end pavilions, was completed in 1863 (Fig 34).

Figure 34
Royal Crescent was initiated in 1826 by Robert Townley on his family's extensive land holdings on the west cliff.
[DP247160]

Harbour improvements

At the turn of the 19th century the harbour trustees completed a range of buildings in the pier yard. Designed by Samuel Wyatt, they included a bonded warehouse, a pier house for the trustees' use and a three-storey harbour master's house. Access to the harbour was controlled by two sets of gates with attached gate lodges. The pier house featured a rusticated entrance hall; on the *piano nobile* was a committee room, 5.8m high with a continuous balcony and an inlaid compass motif set into the floor. Clad in Portland stone, the structure was crowned with a copper-clad cupola. Built at considerable expense, some of those who paid harbour dues regarded it as an indulgence of the trustees.

A clock house was completed *c* 1816 by John Shaw senior (1776–1832), architect to the trustees (Fig 35). In 1819 an astronomical clock by Captain Henry Kater was installed in its vaulted upper room. A brass meridian line was laid in the floor for the correction of ships' chronometers, supervised by the Revd

Figure 35
The clock house is the oldest surviving building commissioned by Ramsgate's harbour trustees. [DP251298]

Figure 36
An early view of the obelisk in the pier yard, probably
taken from the mast of a ship docked on the slipway.
This photograph probably dates from the mid-1860s, as
it shows Ramsgate Harbour station (opened 1863) and
the Coastguard Station (1865–6) but not the Granville
Hotel, which was substantially complete by 1869. Note
the stone yard in the foreground.
[BB97/00002]

Figure 36
An early view of the obelisk in the pier yard, probably
taken from the mast of a ship docked on the slipway.
This photograph probably dates from the mid-1860s, as
it shows Ramsgate Harbour station (opened 1863) and
the Coastguard Station (1865–6) but not the Granville
Hotel, which was substantially complete by 1869. Note
the stone yard in the foreground.
[BB97/00002]

Samuel Vince, Plumian Professor of Astronomy at Cambridge University, who lived at Bellevue House on the east cliff. Flanking wings hosted a warehouse and a carpenter's workshop. Some felt that the construction budget would have been better invested in improvements to the harbour itself. 'I have enquired among the workmen, what it is for', said the shipowner Nathanial Domett at an 1822 parliamentary enquiry. 'There is a dial and a pretty cupola; it is a pretty thing to look at from Sir William Curtis's garden, but I cannot see any use in it'.[80]

Ramsgate's elevated status was affirmed after King George IV embarked for Hanover from the harbour in September 1821, having stayed at Curtis's residence, Cliff House. In November the trustees learned from the Home Secretary, Viscount Addington, that the harbour was henceforth to be denominated a royal harbour and that the royal standard was to be hoisted there on the king's birthday and on the anniversaries of his accession and coronation. An obelisk of red Aberdeen granite, 16m in height, was erected in 1822–3 to commemorate the honour (Fig 36). It was intended to match the proportions of the obelisks at the Temple of Thebes, reflecting the contemporary 'Egyptomania'.

Figure 37
The lighthouse on the west pier symbolised continuing investment on the part of the harbour trustees. A brass figure of peace, bearing an olive branch, was originally mounted on the finial.
[DP247141]

560km away at Dún Laoghaire Harbour in County Dublin lies another granite obelisk, erected in 1823 to commemorate the embarkation of the king in September 1821 and its designation as a royal harbour. John Rennie junior (1794–1874) was the engineer to both harbours.

In 1826 John Shaw senior rebuilt Jacob's Ladder as a flight of stone steps a little to the west of the timber structure. He was also responsible for a powder magazine, installed in 1828 on the west pier and a slipway built a decade later against the inner face of the east pier. The latter featured a steam operated travelling cradle running on inclined rails above granite sets. After concerns that the lighthouse might be struck by vessels entering the harbour, a replacement, 9.5m to the west, was decided upon. Designed by John Shaw junior (1803–70) and completed in 1843 for the sum of £900, the Cornish granite tower bears the Latin motto *perfugium miseris*: refuge for the unfortunate (Fig 37).

Resort infrastructure

While William Henry Ireland, writing in 1828, considered that although the 'finer rows of gentlemen's mansions' on the cliffs were superior to anything Margate had to offer, he reckoned that the town centre was inferior to its rival, its streets being narrow and dirty and lacking squares and open spaces.[81] After the Napoleonic Wars purposeful strides were taken to update the town's civic infrastructure with an eye to enhancing the resort's attractiveness to visitors.

Figure 38
The town hall and market of 1839, situated at the junction of Queen Street and Harbour Street.
[OP29136]

Reform and modernisation were effected through a combination of private enterprise and municipal government in the form of the improvement commissioners.

The first short-lived experiments with coal gas lighting were made by Thomas Sawyer, a chemist in Harbour Street, who rigged up a local circuit of lamps between Harbour and York Streets. But it was not until 1824 that the Isle of Thanet Gas Light and Coke Company was established in pursuance of an Act of Parliament for gas lighting Margate, Ramsgate and Broadstairs. The parish of St Lawrence followed in 1851. Ramsgate's gasworks, erected under the supervision of the gas engineer Joseph Hedley, were originally located just within the town's limits at the junction of Hardres Street and Boundary Road.

The cholera epidemics of the 1830s underscored the urgency of improving the town's water supply, drawn from private wells, rainwater tanks and from the town pump at the Bull and George Inn. Piped water was laid on by the Ramsgate Water Company after a private bill of 1834. Its surveyor James Watson devised a scheme abstracting water from the River Stour to a spring engine house and works at Cliffsend and thence to a reservoir, engine house and works at Southwood, south of St Lawrence. In 1855 a second works was opened at Whitehall. By 1866 it was reported that 78 houses had no water supply, 60 houses drew from rainwater tanks and 277 from wells but the remainder – about 2,000 inhabited houses – were connected to the municipal waterworks.

Further municipal improvement was effected under a second Improvement Act of 1838. The commissioners levied a coal duty to fund the appointment of two street keepers, four firemen and a number of street cleaners. They were also empowered to widen and improve the streets, Chatham Street being a notorious accident black spot. The following year the old market building was replaced with a new town hall and vegetable market. A stucco'd building with a curved front and a broad colonnade to shelter the market stalls, it was designed by William Woodland and built by T A Grundy at a cost of £1,236 (Fig 38). At the laying of the first stone, Peter Burgess, now the senior commissioner, looked forward to a future era 'when our descendants will make use of stone for that which our limited circumstances compel us to effect with brick'.[82] A meat and fish market was erected at York Street to designs by G M Hinds, with a passage leading to the vegetable market.

Yet the regulation of trade continued to represent a source of friction. A flashpoint occurred in July 1839 when, while the markets were still being constructed, the commissioners passed a regulation to prevent 'fish hawkers' selling their wares in the street. After the conviction of nine offenders, a large crowd of fishermen and women assembled and broke into the building where the prisoners were temporarily being held. After facilitating their escape the rioters proceeded to the harbour, 'pausing to groan and hiss at several of the commissioners' houses'.[83] A detachment of the 11th Light Dragoons was called for, but by the time it arrived the chairman of the commissioners had suspended the offending clause.

Worship

With its increasing prominence and population (over 6,000 by 1821), it became clear that Ramsgate needed its own parish, distinct from St Lawrence, and an Anglican place of worship of suitable capacity and prestige to accommodate both inhabitants and seasonal visitors. In October 1823 it was resolved at a general meeting of Ramsgate's citizens to build a new church to seat 2,000, including 1,200 unreserved pews. Land off High Street was purchased for £900 from the Townley family and a design obtained from the architect Henry Hemsley junior (1793–1825). Completed at a cost of £23,034 or £11 9s per sitting, St George's was one of the more expensive of the 'commissioners' churches' built across the country with a parliamentary grant. The commissioners granted £9,000 and loaned a further £13,000, while the inhabitants subscribed £2,000. The lighthouse authority Trinity House contributed £1,000 on the grounds that its lantern tower, based on the Boston stump, would serve as a useful seamark (Fig 39).

Its foundation stone was laid on 30 August 1824 (the same day as Ramsgate was first lit by gas), but construction had still not commenced by the time of Hemsley's death in May 1825. 'Some deviations from the original plan' were made by his successor, Henry Edward Kendall.[84] Erected by the local builders D B Jarman and T A Grundy, the completed church was consecrated by the Archbishop of Canterbury in October 1827. A separate burial ground had been consecrated in 1824 adjoining the liberty boundary, although St George's churchyard was also used for interments.

Figure 39
St George's Church is a prominent symbol of the renewal of Anglicanism in Ramsgate and the town's growing autonomy.
[DP247213]

Figure 40
The Baptist chapel on Cavendish Street attests to a
strong non-conformist presence in the Victorian town.
[DP160397, Patricia Payne]

Non-conformist worship flourished in 19th-century Ramsgate with the opening of chapels serving several denominations. Dissenting worship is recorded from at least 1662 when the vicar of St Laurence, the Revd Peter Johnson, was expelled for refusing to follow the terms of the Act of Uniformity. Initially meeting at a clandestine location on Harbour Street, the congregation later realised a chapel in Queen Street under the ministry of the Revd Pack, replaced in 1743 by the Ebenezer Chapel (also known as the Congregational Church) on Meeting Street. It was replaced in 1838–9 with a larger building designed by G M Hinds and William Woodland and erected by William Saxby, the foundation stone being laid by Mary Townley in her 84th year.

A long-demolished General Baptist Church, bearing the date 1724 existed at Farley Place near the harbour, while in 1810 a Wesleyan Chapel was erected on Hardres Street at a cost of £5,000. It was joined in 1818 by the Zion Chapel, which met at Goldfinch's former concert room. Later and larger was the Baptist Chapel on Cavendish Street, built in 1840 for the Revd John Mortlock Daniell for about £5,000. James Wilson of Bath supplied a remarkable design in a free Romanesque style, sidestepping the denominational associations of the Gothic Revival (Fig 40).

Education

Thanet possessed no public school of ancient foundation, but from the mid-18th century tutelage was offered to Ramsgate's better-off families and its seasonal visitors. Mostly run by women from residential addresses, these small independent schools offered a refined education to a handful of pupils. A boarding school was founded in July 1795 by William Humble, his pupils known locally as 'Humble's bees'. Fees were 20 guineas per annum. The following year Humble purchased property on Love Lane (now Chatham Street), obtaining a mortgage of £1,400 in 1798. By 1809, Chatham House Academy had been extended with two school rooms, one of which 'stands over a colonnade, where, in wet weather, the young gentlemen may enjoy their pastimes uninterrupted by the rain'.[85] The premises was purchased in 1839 by Thomas Whitehead of Margate, the grandfather of the philosopher Alfred North Whitehead.

By 1780 Ramsgate possessed a charity school, supported by voluntary contributions and governed by a committee. In 1811 it moved into a simple, purpose-built school house on Meeting Street, erected at a cost of £2,000 and accommodating around 200 boys and girls. The stuccoed building was in 1864 converted to the Foresters' Hall. In 1808 Joseph Fox of Guy's Hospital travelled to Ramsgate to promote the 'monitorial system' devised by the Quaker educationist Joseph Lancaster. Two Sunday schools were established along these lines, with older or more proficient pupils acting as classroom assistants, passing on what they had learned to younger children. Lancaster's followers, many of them non-conformists, established the British and Foreign School Society, and a nondenominational British School opened in the 1840s next to the Cavendish Baptist Chapel. From 1811 the Church of England promoted a National Society, which provided plain buildings for elementary schooling, subsidised from 1833 by a government grant. Princess Victoria visited Ramsgate's National School during her stay in 1836 when she donated the sum of £200.

Ramsgate Sands *by William Powell Frith (1819–1909) is a social study of the Victorian middle class at play. Frith made preparatory sketches at Ramsgate, where he spent the summer of 1851. The finished painting, also known as* Life at the Seaside, *was exhibited at the Royal Academy in 1854 where it was seen by Queen Victoria, who soon acquired it for the Royal Collection. Ramsgate's seafront provides a background to his seaside scene, including (from left to right) the clock house, Royal Hotel of 1842, obelisk, pier house (with dome), harbour master's house, Pier Castle, Kent Terrace, Victoria Baths (with pediment) and the open-fronted shed of the stone yard. On the east cliff is Albion House (where Victoria stayed in 1835), East Cliff House and Wellington Terrace.*
[Royal Collection Trust / © Her Majesty Queen Elizabeth II 2020, www.rct.uk/collection/405068]

4

Victorian Ramsgate

The railways and mass tourism

On 13 April 1846 the railway age arrived at Ramsgate with the opening of the Canterbury to Ramsgate branch of the South-Eastern Railway Company's London to Dover line. Instead of driving the line through the town, the Ramsgate branch terminated at a neoclassical station on Margate Road (Fig 41). The journey time from the Bricklayers' Arms terminus in London was a little under three hours, and for a short period the company operated a connecting steamboat service to Ostend.

The cheap fares offered by the South-Eastern opened up day trips or weekend excursions to the lower-middle-class and working-class Londoner. From the start, the railway allowed large groups to travel together: in 1848 the directors of the company laid on a special train for 400 workmen employed at the Bricklayers' Arms and Deptford stations, 'with their wives and sweethearts'.[86] In addition to employing a sizable staff of clerks, porters and engineers, the Ramsgate station attracted industry such as the Isle of Thanet Steam Flour Mills (1865, architect E W Pugin) and the South Eastern Works (1867), the latter used by E W Pugin in the manufacture of furniture for his Granville Hotel (see page 97). For the first time, the clerical and professional classes could commute daily to their place of employment, influencing the pace and character of subsequent suburban development.

Visitor numbers dramatically increased throughout the second half of the 19th century and with them, expectations of new forms of entertainment, consumption and accommodation (Fig 42). For some years visitors had complained that little had been done to improve the town's facilities and attractions. In 1846 the *Illustrated London News* concluded that 'great reform is needed at Ramsgate, or the spirit of the visitors will get far before it'.[87] Yet in renewing itself, the resort faced a delicate balance: how to cater for mass tourism without endangering its exclusive, genteel reputation. 'It requires marvellous courage now to confess any interest in places so utterly discarded by fashion as are Margate and Ramsgate', Elizabeth Stone wrote in 1846; 'they are still crowded, but by decidedly unfashionable people'.[88] This was not a new dilemma but the prospect of cheap transport and mass tourism brought the social status of the resort into sharp perspective.

Figure 41
The main entrance to Ramsgate Town station, located at the side of the terminus.
[RO/06952/001]

On 5 October 1863 the Kent Coast Railway's line reached Ramsgate, soon taken over by the London, Chatham and Dover Railway. Part of a branch connecting Faversham with the coastal resorts of north Kent, it reached Ramsgate via a tunnel section *c* 1.5km long, arriving at a new terminus next to the Sands. The seaside station changed the character of the Sands, drawing attention to the social contrast between the 'Cockneyfied' town and the more exclusive venues located at the safe distance of the east and west cliffs:

> The railway makes a background in place of the cliff and the whole intervening space between the land and the bathers seems smaller. Again, this space is unquestionably filled by a different class. Railway facilities and the extreme cheapness of the rate at which people are brought down by boat have told upon the Sands.[89]

When it came to sea bathing, a delicate balance had to be struck between popularity and respectability. Victorian notions of morality account for the persistence of the bathing machine until the First World War (Fig 43). Breaches of Ramsgate's bylaws concerning bathing decorum provoked outraged letters to the London newspapers, but the authorities felt that they were being held to account for the behaviour of their guests:

> It is a well-known fact that ladies in town are not ladies by the sea-side— they apparently leave their good manners at home, for they may be seen disporting themselves while bathing in a manner anything but delicate, and crowding around the bathing machines to gratify a morbid fancy while from the pier and cliffs the bathers are under whole batteries of opera glasses.[90]

Figure 42
A shrimp pot lid depicting fishing vessels (some with lobster pots) at Pegwell Bay. Pegwell Bay was famous for its shrimps which could be purchased fresh or in paste form, the latter sold in coloured earthenware pots. F & R Pratt of Fenton in the Staffordshire Potteries became the leading manufacturer of polychrome transfer printed pot lids, which are today highly collectable.
[DP251324, courtesy of Veronica Pratt]

Figure 43
This hand coloured lantern slide depicts Ramsgate
Sands at the turn of the 20th century. A phalanx of
bathing machines dominate the scene, much as they had
at the beginning of Victoria's reign.
[DP251291; courtesy of Sally and Rob Holden]

Victorian venues

A range of entertainment venues and places of assembly opened in the Victorian period, catering for a wide variety of tastes and audiences of residents and visitors. When St George's Hall on George Street opened in 1849 it was the largest public venue in the town, although not on the scale of the assembly rooms at Margate and elsewhere. The initiative of Edward Bing (1811–71), a builder who lived on George Street, it was designed by G M Hinds in a sober classical style and its cost of £1,200 was defrayed by the sale of shares at £10 each (Fig 44).

Nearby Effingham House was from 1835 the meeting place of the Ramsgate Scientific and Literary Institution. At the rear, facing Guildford Lawn, the United Literary Club built a lecture hall in 1868. This hosted readings and recitals for 'the promotion of amusement and happiness for the working men' and was later remodelled as the headquarters of the Ramsgate Cycling & Motoring Club.[91] Of a similarly 'improving' nature were the Church Institute on Broad Street (1872, W E Smith) and the Christ Church Mission Hall at 41 Royal Road (1880, A R Pite). Exclusive private members' clubs took the place of the old circulating libraries and assembly rooms. West Cliff Mansions, built on the grounds of Cliff House, included the Albion Club (No 2) of 1886 by the ecclesiastical architects Pugin & Pugin and the Temple Yacht Club which opened in 1896, gaining its royal charter the following year (Fig 45).

Music hall and vaudeville acts visited the *Établissement* at Granville Marina (see page 99), the Harp Music Hall on Harbour Parade, the Philharmonic Music Hall at the rear of the Rose of England pub on High Street and St James's Hall on Broad Street. The Alexandra Theatre at 5 Hardres Street opened in May 1869 in the former Zion Chapel, its line-up including the

Figure 44
This photograph shows St George's Hall of 1849. The venue later traded as the Royal Assembly Rooms (in 1897), Shanly's Electric Theatre (from December 1911) and Star Cinema (c 1914–27).
[DP247226]

Figure 45
West Cliff Mansions were developed in the 1880s and
1890s on the site of the gardens of Cliff House, the
sometime residence of Sir William Curtis. The left-hand
building, in red brick, is No 2, the former Albion Club of
c 1886 by Pugin and Pugin. No 5, of 1896, is the Royal
Temple Yacht Club. It is adjoined by No 8, Harbour
House, of 1894–5 by W A McIntosh Valon as the
harbour master's residence.
[DP247181]

lion comique George Leybourne ('the original Champagne Charlie') and Esther Austin's troupe of Parisian carnival dancers.[92] When the proprietor applied to renew his theatre licence, local residents complained about the low character of the venue, frequented by 'fishing apprentices and trawlers, and loose women'.[93] After being gutted by fire it was rebuilt in 1882 as the Victoria Coffee Palace and Temperance Hotel, reflecting the close ties between religion and the temperance movement.

But Ramsgate still lacked a central venue of the scale that could cater for its many hundreds of visitors. The Ramsgate architect William Bridge designed an assembly room for the prominent site on the corner of High Street and George Street but the proposal stalled. No more successful was the consortium of local businessmen who attempted to raise funds to build a large theatre, concert hall and assembly rooms at the bottom of Chatham Street. They were beaten to it by 'Lord' George Sanger (1825–1911), the showman and circus impresario who took over The Hall by the Sea at Margate, the forerunner of Dreamland. In July 1883 he opened Sanger's Amphitheatre on a High Street corner plot (Fig 46).

The Victorian equivalent of a multi-purpose indoor arena, it included a restaurant and shopping parade and was illuminated by eight female statues bearing ornamental gas lamps, modelled on examples Sanger spotted at the Paris Opéra. Albert Latham, Margate's borough surveyor, came up with a flamboyant design he described as 'Sangerian'.[94] In 1908 the amphitheatre was converted by the architect Frank Matcham to the Royal Palace Theatre, and in 1929 it was further adapted for showing films. Most of the complex, including the grand entrance, was demolished in 1961 to make way for a supermarket, leaving the four left-hand bays (50–56 High Street).

Victorian technology brought new types of seaside entertainments. Seaside resorts attracted early commercial photographers, leading the *Photographic News* to describe Ramsgate as 'a paradise of photographers ... It appears to be as much the custom for the ladies who are staying here to have their portraits taken as to take a bath'.[95] Studio portraits and hand-coloured souvenir views could be purchased from studios such as John C Twyman's on High Street. A long-standing preoccupation was how to attract visitors outside the summer season. The winter garden, successfully introduced at Southport, Blackpool, Torquay and Tynemouth, was one method. In 1876 the London architects Pennington and Bridgen drew up plans for a winter garden on the site of the harbour stone yard. This was to include an assembly room, skating rink and aquarium in a building with four campanile towers and a central dome, but the scheme never came to fruition.

Pegwell Bay was in 1875–6 the subject of an ambitious reclamation scheme which had the objective of stabilising the cliff. Completed by James Tatnell, the proprietor of the Clifton Hotel, the project involved the construction of a 215m long sea wall enclosing three acres of land. A tunnel underneath Pegwell Road led to Ravenscliff Gardens, with a skating rink, terrace walk with bandstand and wooden pier, the buildings designed by Pain & Clark of London. The gardens and pier were short-lived, while in 1894, J Passmore Edwards purchased the hotel, converting it to a convalescent home for the Working Men's Club and Institute Union of London.

The Ramsgate Promenade Pier Company was formed in December 1878, looking to emulate the success of the piers of Margate, Blackpool, Brighton and

Figure 46
The main entrance to Sanger's Amphitheatre, photographed from Hardres Street around 1904. The bays to the left of the entrance survive as 50–56 High Street.
[Courtesy of Michael Child]

Figure 47
Ramsgate's Promenade Pier c 1890, featuring a
switchback railway, an early form of roller coaster
installed and operated by Thompson's Patent Gravity
Switchback Company.
[BB84/01825]

Hastings. The wrought iron structure was designed by the engineer Henry
Robinson and constructed by Head Wrightson & Co of Stockton-on-Tees. It
extended from the far end of the Granville Marina and at the pier head were two
refreshment kiosks, later joined by a pavilion. The company struggled to make
the pier pay and from 1888 to 1891 Thompson's Patent Gravity Switchback
Company operated an early form of roller coaster on the deck, only four years
after La Marcus Adna Thompson opened his pioneering switchback railway at
Coney Island, New York (Fig 47). The pier was gutted in 1918 and its
substructure was further damaged by a mine explosion the following year; it was
finally dismantled in 1930.

Public buildings and works

Perhaps Ramsgate's most crucial emergency service was provided by those
keeping watch over its coastal waters. To varying degrees the role has involved
revenue protection, coastal rescue and providing auxiliary functions to the Royal
Navy. A lifeboat station was established in 1802 by the harbour trustees who
commissioned a vessel from the South Shields boatbuilder Henry Greathead. At
the end of the Napoleonic Wars a watch house or 'preventative station' was

established at the base of the east cliff, perhaps part of the coast blockade established in 1817 along the Kent and Sussex coast (Fig 48). It accommodated a commissioned officer and a body of men whose principal task was the prevention of smuggling. The facility was absorbed into the coastguard service but was displaced in the early 1860s with the construction of the Ramsgate Harbour station. Following legislation of 1856 the Admiralty inherited responsibility for maintaining the coastguard service. In 1865–6 a 'show station' was erected on the east cliff, symbolising the regional importance of Ramsgate's coastguard division which oversaw the Thanet coast (Fig 49).[96]

By the mid-century Ramsgate was faced with a combination of population increases, rapid growth and social deprivation. These challenges were bound up with the need to compete with other resorts for a share of the seaside market. The town responded with a patchwork of new amenities and community facilities, often uncoordinated and provided through charitable or voluntary agency. Ramsgate's rapid growth, including an increased electorate, presented problems with which its existing system of local government was

Figure 48
The watch house or preventative station erected at the foot of the east cliff after the Napoleonic Wars. These buildings, with the adjoining shipyard of Messrs Miller, Hinds and Beeching, were cleared to make way for the Kent Coast Railway's line and Ramsgate Harbour terminus, which opened in 1863.
[OP07434]

not devised to cope: reform and increased regulation of trade and development were necessary. With expanded municipal powers and duties came public debates, keenly reported in the local press, about the roles and extent of local government and the way in which it co-existed with older models of funding such as philanthropy, voluntary charities, public subscription and private enterprise.

Seeking additional powers to promote Ramsgate's growth and development, the town's improvement commissioners in 1865 formed a local board under the terms of the 1858 Local Government Act. Their seal of office, drawn up by the Revd John Gilmore, combined a prancing horse (the arms of Kent), a lion and ship conjoined to represent the Cinque Ports, a dolphin to signify a bathing place and a lighthouse for the harbour of refuge, encapsulating 'the whole tale of the town of Ramsgate'.[97] A third Improvement Act of 1878 empowered the commissioners to extend the district to include part of St Lawrence parish and to achieve independence from the jurisdiction of the Cinque Port of Sandwich. Provision was made for a new road linking the east and west cliffs, a long-standing ambition which vied with the improvement of the existing highways. The Borough of Ramsgate was incorporated in March 1884, with a mayor, six aldermen and 18 councillors representing six wards. Its motto was *Salus naufragis salus aegris*: safety for the shipwrecked, health for the sick (Fig 50).

Responsibilities inherited by the local board from the improvement commissioners included the maintenance and improvement of the town's thoroughfares. By 1866 a programme of road widening was underway in High Street and King Street; Queen Street followed. 'Besides obviating the danger to pedestrians and improving the access to the centre of the town from the east cliff and from Broadstairs', the *Thanet Advertiser* claimed, it will no doubt do much to resuscitate the business capabilities of King Street'.[98] But the compensation settlements agreed with property owners tended to be expensive and disputatious.

There were also public buildings to consider. In 1873 the local board resolved to build a police station and constable's house for an estimated cost of £1,250. Their architect, G M Hinds, designed a three-storey house (4a York St) on the site of the old Fish and Meat Market on York Street. An adjacent passageway led to a red-brick and flint station on Charlotte Court, underneath which were six detention cells (Fig 51). The police buildings joined an existing fire station (No 4c) which had been converted in 1868 from the former market buildings. Prior to that, reports of fire were relayed to the police station which summoned Ramsgate's voluntary fire brigade.

Ramsgate's local board was concerned with enhancing the appearance of the public realm and the amenities available to residents and visitors. Gardens, parks and recreation grounds were widely seen as beneficial to public health, enabling working-class residents to participate in 'improving' recreation and adding value to nearby housing developments. Many residents regretted the loss of the town's open spaces to housing. As one concerned citizen put it, 'it has often struck me as remarkable that the residents have seen nearly the whole of the open spaces in the town cut for building purposes, without a word of protest or an effort to preserve for future generations a breathing space for their offspring'.[99] Such was the demand for leisure that in 1869 James Woolcott opened the Pavilion Recreation Ground on a field adjoining Hollicondane

Figure 50
The coat of arms of the Borough of Ramsgate, granted in 1884 and seen here on the gasworks administration building. Based upon the seal of Ramsgate's local board, the escutcheon depicts the white horse of Kent, a lion conjoined to the hulk of a ship, a dolphin and a golden lymphad or galley.
[DP251258]

Figure 51
The police station of 1874 on Charlotte Court, linked to a
contemporaneous constable's house at 4a York Street.
[DP251252]

Tavern, while the so-called 'government acre' west of Grange Road was leased
from the War Office as a public recreation ground.

Under the Public Health Act of 1875 local authorities could fund and
maintain public land for recreation. The newly formed Ramsgate Corporation
started by acquiring and throwing open Ramsgate's communal gardens, most of
which were hitherto open only to residents or subscribers. In 1879 an agreement
was reached with the owners of the Granville Hotel for Victoria Gardens to be

The Fountain, Ellington Park,   Ramsgate.

Figure 52
An early 20th-century postcard showing the ornamental fountain in Ellington Park, supplied by Royal Doulton. It was dismantled in 1945.
[PC10067]

opened free of charge to the public, providing it was lighted at the public expense. Next came the municipalisation of the gardens of Albion Place (1884), Wellington Crescent (1887) and Royal Crescent (1888), while the sunken Italian Gardens east of Royal Crescent were laid out in 1880 at the expense of H J W Johnstone JP. The residue of the Mount Albion estate, including Victoria Gardens and Augusta Stairs was conveyed from the sole surviving trustee to Ramsgate Corporation in 1888. St Luke's Recreation Ground opened in 1893 at a cost of £4,000, serving the expanding districts north of Boundary Road.

Ramsgate still lacked a public park. When in 1892 one of the last undivided parcels of land within the town boundaries came up for auction the corporation was quick to take action. Ellington Park was created in 1893 from the grounds of Ellington House, purchased from the last resident, K W Wilkie. J Cheal & Sons, a Crawley firm of landscape gardeners, devised a picturesque layout with winding paths, a terrace walk in Doultonware and a rustic bandstand (Fig 52). Discussions about converting Ellington House into a reading room and museum came to nothing and it was demolished in February 1893. Salvaged date stones of 1613 and 1649 were incorporated into the facing wall of the terrace walk.

Seafront improvements

Ramsgate's largest civic improvement scheme was completed at the twilight of the Victorian era. It resolved the long-running problem of how to improve the approaches to the cliffs from the harbour, the narrow, steep roads being unsuitable for carriages. Several schemes had been put forward over the years: a marine drive from The Grange to Broadstairs was suggested in 1868, and an open design competition was held in 1878. Neither bore fruit. Finally, in 1890, the borough council approved plans by their engineer, W A McIntosh Valon (1838–1909), which drew upon earlier proposals by their former surveyor W C Barley.

Valon's scheme was inaugurated in November 1891 and completed in 1895 by the contractors William and Thomas Denne of Walmer for a total cost of £56,325. Firstly the quay was widened, a new sea wall built and the inner basin of the harbour deepened. An inclined road, Royal Parade, was constructed against the west cliff towards Nelson Crescent, carried on an arcaded retaining wall into which were let chandler's stores on Military Road (Fig 53). Its design, detailed in red-brick with buff terracotta key stones and roundels, is based on Valon's earlier water tower at Southwood. Above runs the earlier improvement of West Cliff Arcade, a terraced walkway and shopping parade of 1883 by W G Osborne.

At first the eastern carriageway, Madeira Walk, was planned in a straight line running from the bottom of Harbour Street to Albion House. A serpentine route was later adopted to ease the gradient. Valon also changed his mind about how to handle the change in level between the road cutting and Albion Place Gardens. In place of steep banks, which he feared would be difficult to maintain, he devised a gorge of artificial rockwork enclosing both sides of the highway. In 1894 James Pulham & Son of Broxbourne in Hertfordshire contracted to erect rock gardens 'in an artistic, substantial and workmanlike manner' for £770 using Pulhamite, a proprietary blend of cement, sand and other aggregates modelled over a rubble core.[100] The Pulhamite formation is arranged in coloured bands containing crushed shells to resemble geological strata. Fissures and pockets in the rockwork accommodate bedding plants, and elsewhere there are recesses for sheltered seats and tunnels and arched entrances on the south side. A waterfall with rustic bridge, picturesquely sited at a bend of the road, was nicknamed the 'ratepayers' tears' (Fig 54).[101]

Figure 53
Constructed in 1893–5, Royal Parade provided a new approach road from the west cliff to the Royal Harbour. Labour and materials cost some £38,262 in 1895.
[DP251300]

Figure 54
The waterfall at Madeira Walk, part of the landscaping in Pulhamite artificial rockwork.
[DP247252]

Figure 55
The domed roof of the 1894–5 Custom House echoes the
form of the building it replaced, Wyatt's pier house.
[DP251297]

The construction of the approach roads necessitated the rebuilding of several properties on Harbour Parade. At the narrowest part of the quay the Admiral Harvey and the Clarence Baths were redeveloped on a new building line. The Albion Hotel was demolished on the expiry of its lease and in its place the National Provincial Bank (No 50; 1896, W W Gwyther) sets out the curve of Madeira Walk. An agreement was reached with the brewers Tomson and Wotton for the rebuilding of the Shipwright Arms (No 88; 1893), the Alexandra Hotel (No 70; 1907) and the Queen's Head (No 78; *c* 1908).

One of the boldest gestures of Ramsgate's turn-of-the-century renewal was the sweeping away of the range containing Wyatt's pier house, harbour master's house and warehouses, and its replacement in 1894–5 with a new custom house, designed under Valon (Fig 55). Of rich orange-red brick with carved and moulded decoration in a Renaissance revival style, it was crowned with a domed roof and cupola. A site overlooking the western approach was chosen for the harbour master's residence (8 West Cliff Mansions), built in 1894–5 by the contractors Amos & Foad.

Safety for the shipwrecked, health for the sick: health and welfare

Parochial poor relief was supplemented by charitable organisations such as the Margate and Ramsgate Philanthropic Institutions which first met in 1839. A soup kitchen 'for the industrious poor' was organised in winter 1849. It occupied a small single-storey building which still stands on Church Road, next to the church hall.

The care of shipwrecked mariners was another long-standing concern but only in the mid-19th century were facilities organised through philanthropic enterprise. It is said that A W N Pugin rented a property on King Street for use as a Catholic hospital for shipwrecked mariners, assisted by his doctor James Daniel. In 1849 a Seamen's Infirmary was established through the initiative of the Revd E Hoare of Christ Church. Designed by W E Smith 'in the Grecian style', it was opened in May 1850 by the institution's president J A Warre (Fig 56).[102] In 1878 it was supplemented by the Sailors' Home and Harbour Mission on Military Road (page 86).

The Ramsgate and St Lawrence Dispensary was founded in 1820 to provide medical care for those inhabitants who could not afford to pay doctors. In 1876 it admitted 2,022 patients, about one in ten of the population of the two parishes. A single-storey dispensary was erected in Broad Street the following year, its cost of £737 paid by subscription. It was designed by G M Hinds in a fastidious Gothic Revival style influenced by E W Pugin.

Under the terms of the 1872 Public Health Act the improvement commissioners were constituted as an urban sanitary authority and tasked with the provision of public health services. Dr James William Barry was appointed medical officer of health at an annual salary of £50. Not only were the medical officers responsible for the prevention of infectious diseases, they were also sanitary inspectors, indirectly initiating the reform of housing, water supply, sewerage and the removal of public nuisances.

The overcrowded and insanitary conditions of the poorest houses presented the inspectors with a dilemma: they had a duty to condemn insanitary dwellings but no legal powers to rehouse evicted families; furthermore, it was often deemed the tenant's responsibility to render a house fit for habitation, with the owner receiving little or no sanction. In 1878 Barry inspected Rural Place, a row

Figure 56
The Seamen's Infirmary of 1849 on West Cliff Road. Its
cost of £1,396 was met by public subscription.
[DP251254]

Figure 56
The Seamen's Infirmary of 1849 on West Cliff Road. Its
cost of £1,396 was met by public subscription.
[DP251254]

of five early 19th-century cottages on Boundary Road. One three-roomed dwelling was occupied by a family of ten:

> He found the house to be of wooden structure, and with no means of proper ventilation, there being no back windows, and it was a back-to-back house, allowing no current of air to pass between. ... The two rooms used for sleeping purposes were both in a dirty and dilapidated condition. There was no gutter for drainage, and in all probability would render the floor wet and unhealthy.[103]

The local board compulsorily acquired the private water and gas companies under the Improvement Act of 1877 at a cost of £73,539 and £70,000 respectively. A new gasworks site was established east of Boundary Road, marked by a red-brick and terracotta administration building of 1899–1900

designed by Arthur Valon, the 27-year-old son of the borough engineer
(Fig 57). The water works at Southwood were overhauled with a prominent
water tower of 1881, by the engineers Stevenson & Valon, while the engineer
also oversaw a new pumping station which opened in 1898 at Whitehall to
the north.

Curiously for a resort which marketed the restorative properties of its air
and sea water, drainage and sewerage were last to be overhauled. Down to the
mid-19th century, individual cesspits were dug into the chalk aquifers, polluting

Figure 57
*In 1899–1900 Ramsgate Corporation completed this
substantial office and depot for Ramsgate Gasworks. It
is today the only surviving structure on the gasworks
site and awaits a new use.*
[DP251256]

the groundwater supply. In the 1860s and 1870s the town's network of sewers was overhauled and most houses connected to it. The outstanding problem remained the main sewer outfall near the west pier which was exposed at low tide, with sewage washed into the harbour and the Sands with the tide. 'Such an arrangement is an abomination', *The Lancet* protested in 1876, but a new outfall was not laid until 1887.[104]

Schooling

From 1833, the government provided financial assistance to voluntary bodies in erecting new school buildings. In November 1840 St George's National Schools were opened on Church Road on land given by the vicar. The symmetrical layout included girls' and boys' classrooms, each opening onto a large playground, and accommodation for the school master and mistress at the front. It was supplemented by church schools linked to Christ Church (of 1848 on Royal Road) and Holy Trinity (of 1858 on Hereson Road), both designed by W E Smith.

A Ragged School was established in 1849 at Brunswick Place to provide basic literacy, religious instruction and vocational training in response to increasing poverty and unemployment in the town. Within a decade it had moved to premises in Sussex Street purchased by the landowner and MP John Ashley Warre (1787–1860). Evening classes were attended by around 60 girls and boys between 10 and 18 years, some of whom were deemed to be 'in a deplorable state of wretchedness and ignorance'.[105] It was supplemented by a Wesleyan Infant School which opened in 1847 at Newcastle Hill, an area of notorious slums.

The majority of Ramsgate's ratepayers were opposed to establishing a school board under the 1870 Education Act and instead the Anglican, nonconformist and Catholic churches pledged to improve the scope and quality of voluntary education. Under the Act churches could apply for government grants to finance new buildings. In 1875 a schoolhouse and church were erected to designs by W E Smith to serve the new parish district of St Luke's. The school accommodated 150 children and cost £462, its site donated by William Farley, a local builder and developer.

Chatham House School, Ramsgate's longest-established educational institution, was rebuilt in 1879–82 under the direction of the headmaster and owner, the Revd E Gripper Banks. His architect Aaron Twyman devised a long range of orange-red-brick in an English Gothic style somewhat reminiscent of the early London board schools (Fig 58). The headmaster's residence was located at the centre, while boarders were accommodated in partitioned first-floor dormitories in the flanking wings. The privileged category of 'parlour boarders' paid higher fees for a room of their own on the second floor. In 1884 the school gained playing fields through the purchase of part of the grounds of Townley Castle to the north. The range was set back on a new building line in accordance with the corporation's street improvement, while the enterprising Banks also engaged Twyman to build the half-timbered premises to the south (99–107 High Street).

Such was the demand for private education that two purpose-built boys' boarding schools opened nearby on Ellington Road. The first, Aberdeen House School (No 68), was established in 1881 by the Revd George Simmers (Fig 59). He instructed his architect, A R Pite 'to provide a school house so thoroughly domesticated in its arrangements that the dominant idea to the boys should be that of a comfortable home with all its accessories'.[106] The result indeed could be mistaken for a rectory or a large suburban residence, and the influence of A W N Pugin is evident in the compact plan and picturesque, bargeboarded exterior. In 1879 the short-lived Hadleigh House School opened on the corner of South Eastern Road, designed by the Ramsgate architect William George Osborne (1841–1901) for the headmaster Harry Warren.

Thanet proved an attractive location for fee-paying schools of a religious character. As early as 1845, the Baptist minister the Revd John Mortlock Daniell founded a school at Dumpton Hall between Ramsgate and St Peter's 'for the education of the sons of ministers of the gospel of all denominations'.[107] Not far distant was South Eastern College (renamed St Lawrence College in 1906), established in 1879 by the South-Eastern Clerical and Lay Church Alliance, an Evangelical body. A prefabricated iron school house was put up in 1881, followed in 1884 by the first of several phases of red-brick buildings. Designed by W G Osborne, this crenelated and turreted structure originally housed the headmaster's house and dining hall block.

Figure 58
Chatham House School of 1879–82. Designed by Aaron Twyman, the range included a chapel, workshops, laboratories, gymnasium, laundry, sanatorium and assembly hall as well as classrooms and dormitories.
[DP247254]

Figure 59
With its domestic appearance, Aberdeen House School
of 1880 fits comfortably into the setting of the
predominantly residential Ellington estate.
[DP247310]

A Jewish community

Jewish residents are recorded at Ramsgate from the 18th century and a community flourished from the 1840s. This was sustained by connections with the London congregations and the resort's popularity with Jewish families from the east end of London, which was such that kosher food was available from certain grocers.

Ramsgate's most celebrated Jewish resident was the financier and philanthropist Sir Moses Montefiore (1784–1885). He first visited the town in 1822, renting East Cliff Lodge which he purchased in 1831 for £5,500. Decimus Burton was engaged to enlarge and improve the house and its 24-acre estate, and in 1832 Montefiore purchased a vinery at an estate auction at Bretton Hall, West Yorkshire. It had been erected there some seven years earlier by the glasshouse specialists Bailey of Holborn. Montefiore had it transported to

Ramsgate and carefully reassembled against the wall of the stable block (Fig 60). East Cliff Lodge was demolished in 1953 but its vinery, stable block and gatehouse survive.

In 1831 Montefiore founded a synagogue on land adjoining the East Cliff Lodge estate. It was built at a cost of £1,600 to designs by David Mocatta (1806–82), a pupil of Sir John Soane (Fig 61). Stuccoed and neoclassical in style, it was the first synagogue in Britain to be designed by a Jewish architect. In 1864 it was joined by a mausoleum, modelled on the Tomb of Rachel near Bethlehem and intended as a final resting place for his wife Judith. Nearby Montefiore added a theological college to her memory. Built in 1865–9 to the design of Henry David Davis, it was a red-brick crescent in the Elizabethan style with diaperwork and shaped gables.

In 1837 Montefiore built Temple Cottage as accommodation for the ministers at the synagogue. There the brothers the Revd Emanuel Hyman and the Revd Isaac Henry Myers established a school admitting Jewish and Gentile pupils. It was later continued by Isaac's son-in-law Jacob Tritsch at the nearby Hereson House. In 1890 a boarding school for Jewish boys was established at

Figure 60
The so-called Italianate glasshouse at the East Cliff Lodge estate, now within the King George VI Memorial Park. Manufactured by W and D Bailey of Holborn, it was initially installed at the Bretton Hall estate in West Yorkshire and purchased by Moses Montefiore in 1832. [DP114491, Peter Williams]

Figure 61
Montefiore Synagogue, designed by David Mocatta and built in 1831–3. The domed structure is the Mausoleum of Sir Moses and Judith, erected in 1864.
[PLB/N020009]

Townley Castle by Simcha Henry Harris, formerly headmaster of the Jews' Orphan Asylum at Norwood, south London.

Sir Joseph Sebag-Montefiore (1822–1903), Sir Moses's nephew and the inheritor of East Cliff Lodge, continued his philanthropic activities, building six 'model cottages' on Hereson Road in 1887–8. Named Florry Cottages in memory of his late daughter Sarah Floretta, these were offered rent free to three 'respectable and deserving' Jewish families and three Gentile families of similar character.[108] In 1917 Alderman Lazarus Hart, Ramsgate's first Jewish mayor, bequeathed to Ramsgate Corporation a site on Thanet Road and endowed it with £10,000 with which to complete ten 'havens of rest' for persons of any age and sex, five belonging to the Jewish faith and five non-Jews. These were designed by the Ramsgate architect William Everard Healey (1869–1946) 'in 16th century style' and built in 1922–3.[109]

In 1872 Ramsgate's Jewish community determined to establish a private Jewish cemetery. The initiative was led by Benjamin Norden who purchased a freehold plot, previously part of Hollicondane Farm. The cemetery contains both upright Ashkenazi and flat Sephardi gravestones, and is entered through a prayer hall or *ohel* adjoining the cemetery wall.

Pugin and Catholic worship

In the 1840s Ramsgate became a national centre of the Catholic revival due to the efforts of the architect Augustus Welby Northmore Pugin (1812–52). A sense of faith and moral purpose lay behind his pioneering attempt to return to the principles of medieval ecclesiastical architecture. Pugin was attracted to Ramsgate on the basis of a mixture of personal associations (his mother's sister lived at Rose Hill Cottage) and religious ones, chiefly its associations with St Augustine of Canterbury. He took lodgings at Ellington Cottage at the top of Grange Road, where his eldest son Edward Welby Pugin (1834–75) was born. After a period in Salisbury, Pugin returned, staying at Plains of Waterloo where he completed his treatise *The True Principles of Pointed or Christian Architecture* (1841).

In 1843 Pugin bought a plot on the west cliff from the Townley family. There he projected 'not a Grecian villa but a most substantial catholic house not very large but convenient & solid & there is every prospect of a small church on the same ground'.[110] The Grange (1843–4) is an austere, restlessly asymmetrical house of yellow brick, dominated by the tower from which Pugin kept watch in stormy weather for ships in distress (Fig 62). The compact layout was radical, with the principal rooms informally gathered around a double-height entrance hall. Pugin's interior has now been restored with the re-creation of his armorial wallpapers and stained pine joinery, to unexpectedly warm and colourful effect.

Soon after moving in Pugin secured the neighbouring plot and gradually constructed a church, cloister, sacristy, school and priest's house. St Augustine's Church (1845–51) was conceived not as a family chapel but as a Catholic church for Ramsgate. It was a courageous decision at a time when the re-establishment of the Catholic hierarchy in England prompted widespread anti-Catholic sentiment. By funding the works with over £20,000 of his own money, Pugin

Figure 62
This 2018 photograph, taken from an aerial drone, shows the Catholic community founded on the west cliff by A W N Pugin. Clockwise from bottom right are St Augustine's Church of 1845–51; The Grange of 1843–4 and St Edward's Presbytery of 1850–1; and, north of St Augustine's Road, St Augustine's Abbey of 1860–1 and later by E W Pugin.
[John Miller, courtesy of Landmark Trust]

gained control over the smallest details. 'I have never had the chance of producing a single fine, ecclesiastical building', he observed, 'except my own church, where I was both paymaster and architect'.[111] At considerable expense he purchased a strip of land from his arch-rival Matthew Habershon (1789–1852) who, much to Pugin's chagrin, erected Chartham Terrace on the neighbouring plot in 1850–1.

Pugin intended St Augustine's to take its place amongst the country churches of Thanet. Its severe exterior is made up of knapped-flint masonry dressed with bands of Whitby stone unbroken by buttresses. Fish-scale tiles add texture to the roof while a crossing tower, its intended spire never added, echoes the lookout tower of The Grange. Inside, walls of ashlared stone are enriched with stained glass, encaustic tiles, ironwork and intricately carved stone, works of applied art designed by Pugin and executed by his most trusted collaborators (Fig 63). If The Grange provided a model for a medium-sized Victorian house, then St Augustine's represents a landmark in the revival of English Gothic architecture.

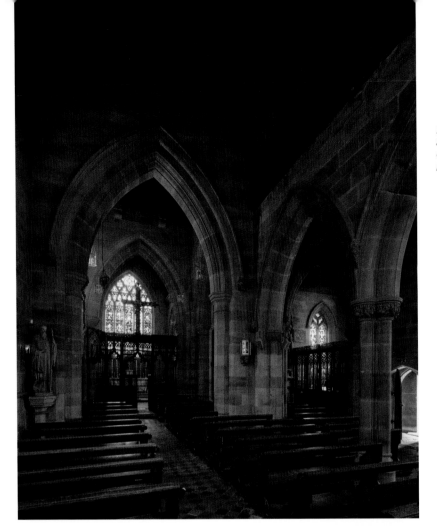

Figure 63
St Augustine's Church: a view from the nave looking east towards the chancel and Pugin chantry.
[DP247167]

Figure 64
The south and west ranges of St Augustine's Abbey, showing the toothed brick arches and deep bargeboards characteristic of E W Pugin's architectural style.
[DP247169]

In 1849 Pugin purchased land on the other side of the road, planning to extend his fledgling Catholic community with a monastery. This was realised after his death with the construction of the Benedictine Abbey of St Augustine, endowed by his friend, the Catholic convert, Alfred Luck. Built in 1860–1, it was designed by E W Pugin in a High Victorian Gothic style which owes more to continental models than does his father's work (Fig 64). To the north he added St Gregory's, a large house for Luck, which in 1867 became the core of the abbey school. A Benedictine convent and school was established on a site north of the Pegwell Road. Just the gateway and walls survive of the original buildings, designed by Whelan and Hayes of London and completed in 1872.[112]

Ramsgate's Catholic settlement hugged the west cliff until 1901–2 when the Church of Saints Ethelbert and Gertrude was built on Hereson Road, 'intended for the Roman Catholic poor of the neighbourhood' (Fig 65).[113] Its designer Peter Paul Pugin (1851–1904), the youngest son of A W N Pugin, envisaged a chancel and tower but these were never completed. In 1928–9 it was joined by a Catholic elementary school designed by W Everard Healey on the 'quadrangle, open-verandah system'.[114] A central playground was enclosed by three single-storey ranges, each entered from a veranda, reflecting the influence of the Edwardian schools designed by John Hutchings of Staffordshire and George Widdows of Derbyshire.

Figure 65
ss Ethelbert and Gertrude on Hereson Road is a late work by Peter Paul Pugin (1851–1904). The photograph shows the lady chapel on the south side of the nave, with its flowing tracery and Latin inscription.
[DP247169]

Anglican expansion

As the town expanded beyond its early footprint, subscriptions were raised for new churches to serve the newly created districts. Holy Trinity, of 1844–5, was a joint initiative of Augusta Emma d'Este (1801–66), the developer of the Mount Albion estate, who donated the land and the Revd G W Sicklemore, who organised a public subscription. Designed by Stevens & Alexander of London, the church cost £3,000 and accommodated 770 worshippers. Conceived in an anti-Catholic climate, Christ Church (1846–8) was intended to counter the local influence of A W N Pugin. A design was procured from the Gothic Revival architect (Sir) George Gilbert Scott (1811–78) and built by William Saxby senior (c 1787–1861), the owner of the western portion of the Vale (Fig 66).

St Paul's, of 1873–4 by Robert Wheeler of Tunbridge Wells, was a mission church in King Street, an area bordered by some of Ramsgate's most overcrowded and insanitary housing. Like Holy Trinity, it was erected by W E Smith. The church was soon enlarged but after being damaged by wartime bombing it was demolished in 1959. The outline of its apse is preserved in the boundary wall to 126 King Street.

Ramsgate's churchmen and its leading citizens were keen to safeguard the moral and spiritual welfare of mariners, not only resident seamen but visitors to the port and shipwrecked men rescued from the Goodwin Sands. The Revd James Eustace Brenan, vicar of Christ Church conceived a floating church moored at the harbour, but through the harbour master obtained a site on Military Road. There W E Smith designed a Sailors' Home and Harbour Mission, opened in July 1878 by Marquis Conyngham. Over the simple church was a hostel which included a dining hall and dormitory with 24 bed cubicles. The uppermost floor served as a 'drying place for the clothing of the shipwrecked men'.[115]

Brennan next organised the building of a Smack Boys' Home on the neighbouring site in 1880–1 (Fig 67). This hostel for the young crew of the local fishing smacks operated until 1915. It was reported that 'all the internal fittings will be of the simplest and most substantial character, suited to the rough habits of the boys, who will be encouraged to regard the building as their home'.[116] Its architect, A R Pite, went on to design the Royal Sailors' Rest, a hostel and bethel funded by the Royal British and Foreign Sailors' Society (Fig 68).

By 1869 it was clear that the town's burial grounds were full and that a cemetery was required. A burial board was constituted, 20 acres of rising ground on the east cliff was purchased, and George Gilbert Scott junior (1839–97) was commissioned to design the cemetery chapels and lodge (Fig 69). The grounds were laid out by A Markham Nesfield, and Scott's buildings, in a late English Gothic style, were completed in 1871–2. Some perceived the young man's appointment as a snub to the Ramsgate-based E W Pugin, who may have been behind this anonymous protest published in the *Thanet Advertiser*:

> To my utter astonishment I hear the name of Gilbert Scott associated with our new cemetery. How is this? Have we not one at home of equal, if not of greater reputation, who would not only do all that could be done to vindicate *art*, but who has always displayed a generosity most unworthily accepted by, Yours lamenting, 'Ramsgate'[117]

Figure 66
A view of Christ Church from the balcony of 20 Vale Square (originally 2 Vale Villas). Its tall spire is clad with wooden shingles.
[DP251329]

Figure 67 (above, right)
The Ramsgate Home for Smack Boys opened in 1881, providing shelter for the lads apprenticed to the fishing smack skippers of the Ramsgate fleet. To the left is the earlier Sailors' Home and Harbour Mission. [DP247158]

Figure 68 (above)
The Royal Sailors' Rest makes a distinguished Edwardian contribution to the seafront. Its site was previously occupied by the seawater baths established in 1790 by Joseph Dyason. [DP251265]

Figure 69 (right)
For Ramsgate Cemetery George Gilbert Scott junior designed a double chapel in an English late Gothic style, with non-conformist and Anglican mortuary chapels separated by a tower. [DP251311]

Victorian housing

By the start of Victoria's reign, Ramsgate's oldest established streets and its seafront were almost fully built-up (Fig 70). New developments of any ambition had to exploit the few remaining parcels of open land in the centre or the open fields beyond the Liberty Way. The grandest houses were built on the west and east cliffs for wealthy citizens, visitors and retirees. In the middle of the 19th century demand rose for middle-class villas for the burgeoning professional and business class. Many of Ramsgate's poorest inhabitants occupied the early and ramshackle housing near the harbour and the area around King Street which was soon earmarked for redevelopment.

The construction of the railway in the 1840s encouraged local landowners to build modest terraced houses off Margate Road and Boundary Road for railway and industrial workers. The new station changed the character of its immediate area and marked the premature end of Victoria Crescent, a genteel scheme of 1833–5 by Wildish and Grundy, after only three villas (3–7 Park Road) had been realised. It took time for the railway's influence to spread, facilitating middle-class housing developments on agricultural land in St Lawrence parish. Suburban growth was a gradual and relatively uncoordinated process, evidenced by the 'ugly outskirts of Ramsgate' with their 'spoilt gardens, half-made roads [and] half-built streets'.[118]

The prospect of the railway attracted a few London investors from the 1830s onwards when it was first discussed. Ramsgate Vale was a development by the London hosier James Creed Eddels (1796–1857), who in 1839 purchased a five-acre field behind West Cliff Road. Victoria Terrace (1–9 Vale Square) seems to have gone up first, forming the eastern range of a long central square. On the north and south sides Eddels opted for the up-to-the-minute format of detached and paired villas (Fig 71). 'There is much demand for detached villas by those who having ceased to labour, and who wish to find a haven wherein to end their days in peace', reported the *South Eastern Gazette* in 1850.[119] The Vale's villas were built to order by William Saxby and others in an assortment of styles including Gothick (Claremont, No 48), Tudorbethan (Albert Villa, No 49) and Greek revival (No 50). Scott's Christ Church crowned the development.

A contemporary scheme was West Cliff Terrace (*c* 1843–5), a big-boned Italianate terrace standing amongst the corn fields off Pegwell Road. Here the

Figure 70
G M Hind's 1849 map of Ramsgate was a revision of a map of 1822 by R. Collard and G. Hurst of Broadstairs. [Courtesy of Michael Child]

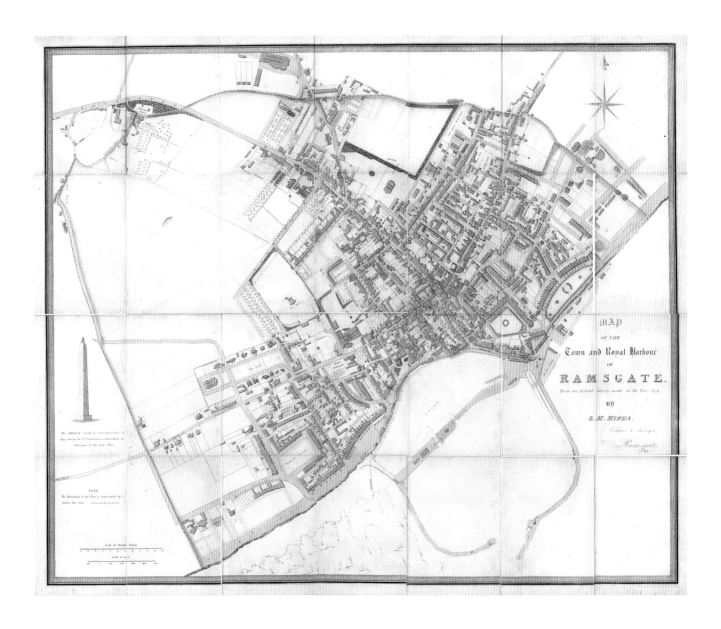

Figure 71
The Vale offered a new type of residential development
in Ramsgate: secluded, inward facing and developed at
a lower density than was hitherto common.
[DP247232]

Figure 72
Guildford Lawn was built in the early 1840s by William
Saxby senior, a Ramsgate carpenter and builder.
Note the wider windows of the south-facing houses.
[DP247295]

prime mover was W H Stamp, the Secretary to the London Gas Light Company, who employed the London architect John Stevens.[120] Later the property passed into the hands of Stamp's solicitor, Alderman David Williams Wire, sometime Mayor of London.

The gardens, orchards and ropewalks north of Queen Street provided an increasingly sought-after source of prime building land. Guildford Lawn was erected in the early 1840s by William Saxby on Brimstone's orchard, west of George Place (Fig 72). Named after the Earl of Guilford, Lord Warden of the Cinque Ports, this L-shaped terrace is an early Victorian building in Regency dress, with prominent bow windows finished in white render. Construction was then a hazardous and unregulated operation:

> An accident occurred from the breaking of the puttock [putlog] of a scaffolding at the buildings in Guildford Lawn, Ramsgate, erecting by Mr Saxby; when Thomas Miller, bricklayer, and his labourer, fell into the area, a distance of nearly 30 feet [9m], without loss of life or breaking bones, but they were seriously hurt by the fall. At the same time Mr William Saxby, son of the builder, was on the scaffold, but fortunately caught hold of the gutter, and then hung on some time, until extricated from his perilous situation.[121]

Figure 73
Early Victorian villas on West Cliff Road, built on land sold by the miller Henry George Thornton. From left to right: No 38, Oscar Villa of c 1837 by G M Hinds for Magnus Gibson; No 40 of c 1840 for William Lewis; Nos 42–44 of c 1850.
[DP247241]

Nearby Cavendish Street was laid out *c* 1840 by William Woodland and
T A Grundy, connecting Queen Street and George Place. Their road took its
name from the Baptist chapel there and gained further prestige from grand
residences such as Cavendish House and the double-pile Cavendish Villas. At
the same time Woodland and Grundy widened George Place, rebuilding the
George and Dragon pub on the corner (Nos 31–5) for Tomson's brewery.

In 1838 the miller Henry George Thornton, who owned three windmills on
Grange Road, attempted to develop some of his land along what is today known
as West Cliff Road. Only a few scattered houses had been built west of the
brewery. He divided the frontages into building plots 'to be called West Cliff
Terrace' and put them up for auction. Purchasers had the option of choosing
'designs of such houses as each plot is well adapted to' drawn up by his architect,
Hezakiah Marshall of Canterbury.[122] Only three detached villas transpired,
including the elegant but stylistically conservative Oscar Villa (No 38) by
G M Hinds (Fig 73).

Further development did not diminish the road's exclusive reputation which
by 1862 was 'fast becoming the Belgravia of Ramsgate'.[123] Edward Bing was

Figure 74
*Camden Place (1–12 La Belle Alliance Square) of c 1835
features balconies recessed behind unusually wide
elliptical arches.*
[DP251233]

Figure 75
East Court, by architects Sir Ernest George and Harold
Peto, brought the vernacular revival style to the seaside.
Drawings of the house were exhibited at the 1893 World
Fair at Chicago.
[DP251110]

active here, putting up both middle-class terraces (e.g. Cambridge Terrace, 75–95 West Cliff Road, of 1866–7) and more modest 'two up, two down' versions such as Albert Terrace, 21–35 Albert Street, of 1862. Both feature polychromatic brick decoration and Bing's patented safety sashes, which allowed windows to be cleaned and painted from the inside.

On the east cliff, development behind Wellington Crescent and Albion Place was halting and mixed in character. In 1833 a new road was cut through the back plots, giving access from Clover Hill to Plains of Waterloo. Two new squares were laid out in connection with it. Camden Square was likely named after John Jeffreys Pratt, Marquis Camden (1759–1840) while *La Belle Alliance* takes its name from the Belgian farmhouse at which the two victorious field marshals met in the aftermath of the Battle of Waterloo. Camden Place (1–12 La Belle Alliance Square) is notable for the unconventional feature of recessed first-floor balconies set under elliptical arches of gauged brickwork (Fig 74).

Speculative builders sometimes faced claims of jerry building, putting up defective buildings for a quick profit. One house owner alerted prospective purchasers to 'structures which often fall down before completion, quickly display cracked window arches, sinking foundations, rising damps, smokey chimneys, stopped drains, shrunk woodwork, leaky roofs, and other minor evils'.[124] In response to such defects the improvement commissioners adopted bylaws regulating such matters as foundations, the construction and thicknesses of walls, building lines, ventilation, drainage and open space.

At the other end of the social scale, a few grand residences were erected for wealthy retirees on the few remaining seafront sites on the cliffs. East Court, far along the east cliff, was built in 1889–90 by the architects Sir Ernest George and Harold Peto for Sir William Henry Wills (1830–1911), later Baron Winterstoke (Fig 75). One of Kent's finest Arts & Crafts houses, it commands its exposed corner site with clusters of gables hung with green Westmoreland slates and tall red-brick chimneys. Of equal scale is Courtstairs on Pegwell Road, a detached house of 1892 for the brewer Martin J R Tomson. Designed by H G Bailey in a curious Tudorbethan style, the house takes its name from the ancient route descending to Pegwell Bay. To the north was Abbey Gate, a house of *c* 1900 for W G Page, a long-established grocer and wine merchant. It was redeveloped in the 1970s and today only its stable and coach house remains.

The Mount Albion estate and the Granville Hotel

The most ambitious – and riskiest – resort development schemes occurred on the landed estates and farms adjoining the town. One of the first examples was the Mount Albion estate on the east cliff, owned by the family of Lady Augusta Murray (1768–1830). After her 1792 marriage to Prince Augustus Frederick, the sixth son of George III, was declared legally void, the couple parted in 1800 and Lady Augusta retained custody of the couple's two children who took the surname d'Este. In 1807 she purchased a house or pair of houses on the Liberty Way which became Mount Albion House (they survive in a much-altered form, as 22–24 Victoria Road). To it was added about 16 acres of adjoining land, entered from King Street via a gated carriage drive and lodge, today Artillery Road. This was laid out as landscaped parkland, described as 'new pleasure ground' in 1819 (Fig 76).[125] Between the house and its grounds ran the Liberty Way, and in 1820 Lady Augusta applied to the vestry to divert the right of way along the rear of her property.

Figure 76
An extract from Collard and Hurst's 1822 map of
Ramsgate, showing the Mount Albion estate of Lady
Augusta Murray.
[Courtesy of Michael Child]

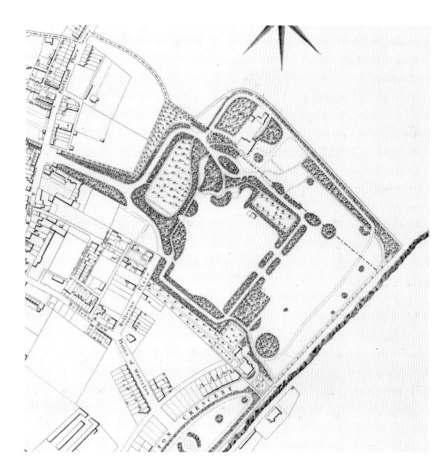

In 1829 Lady Augusta conveyed her real estate to her daughter Augusta
Emma d'Este who, having failed to sell it off in its entirety, divided it up into
building plots which were put up for auction in August 1838. She commissioned
a layout from the architect Thomas Allason (1790–1852), surveyor to the
Ladbroke estate in North Kensington. Mount Albion House was framed by two
broad roads lined with bay-windowed houses. To the rear he envisaged a
London-style square complete with a colonnaded church (eventually realised in
a Gothic Revival style as Holy Trinity Church), while the north-eastern portion
of the estate was taken up with paired villas. Along the seafront ran Albion

Terrace, two rows of grand houses overlooking pleasure grounds and a promenade named Victoria Parade. Augusta Stairs, a flight of stone steps leading down to the Sands, were designed by Allason and built in 1839 at a cost of £850.

Augusta Road was developed earliest, with elegant terraces put up by W E Smith on land purchased by his father, James Smith (Fig 77). On one of the choicest seafront plots Allason built Augusta Lodge as a summer residence for his family. Along the south-east side of Arklow Square (named after a barony conferred upon Prince Augustus in 1801) was built not a terrace as Allason intended but three detached villas, presumably a more profitable or saleable arrangement. Two were developed *c* 1841 by John Gutch to designs by his brother George Gutch (*c* 1791–1874), surveyor to the Bishop of London's estate

Figure 77
These elegant terraced houses on Augusta Road were developed by the Ramsgate builder W E Smith in the 1840s. To the left is Arklow Square and the Church of Holy Trinity.
[DP247239]

Figure 78
The neoclassical Augusta Villa of c 1840 is perhaps the earliest surviving development of the Mount Albion estate. The house was listed at grade II in 2019.
[DP247249]

at Paddington, in which capacity he was probably known to Allason. The social reformer Elizabeth Fry died at the long-demolished Arklow Villa in October 1845. Its neighbour Augusta Villa (25 Bellevue Road) survives, a white rendered house in a pared-back neoclassical style (Fig 78). Along Victoria Road, George Gutch developed Wingham Lodge, which became the seaside residence of Earl Cowper of Panshanger, Hertfordshire.

Buyers remained cautious, so to accelerate the pace of development Allason and his successors made several revisions to the layout. The opening of Ramsgate Harbour station in 1863 made the east cliff a more attractive investment prospect, and the seafront plots were purchased in 1867 by E W Pugin and his business associates. It was one of several joint ventures in which Pugin acted not only as architect but as co-developer. By entering into partnerships he was able to circumvent the rules of the Royal Institute of British Architects which prohibited architects from acting as developers. He started cautiously, completing 3–5 Victoria Parade in the same stuccoed Italianate style as the two existing houses to the west, perhaps bound by a deed of stipulations. Not long after, he commenced a grand terrace of eight substantial houses on the neighbouring plot, very much in his own style.

Figure 79
This 1868 photograph shows E W Pugin's newly-completed Granville Hotel. The development started life as a row of eight palatial houses, as suggested by the separate entrances and pair of steps to the left. To the right, a balcony takes the place of entrance steps, hinting at Pugin's decision to complete the building as a hotel.
[RIBA Collections]

By the end of 1868 Pugin had established the St Lawrence-on-Sea Hotel and Bathing Company. St Lawrence-on-Sea was to be an exclusive suburban resort on the east cliff after the manner of Cliftonville or Westgate-on-Sea, both beside Margate. Part way through construction the terrace was converted into the Granville Hotel, named in honour of the second Earl Granville, Lord Warden of the Cinque Ports (Fig 79). Opened in July 1869, the Granville aimed to bring the luxuries of the aristocracy within the reach of the middle classes. Over the entrance was inscribed 'Through this wide gate / none can come too early, none depart too late'. Facilities included a smoking saloon, billiard room, a ballroom with a stage for performances and a suite of saline spa baths, said to be frequented by the architect himself. Pugin designed the fittings, wallpaper and furniture, which was manufactured at his South Eastern Works on Margate Road.

In its scale and appearance, the new hotel hinted at the hubris of Pugin's venture. It was not to everyone's taste. The architect J P Seddon wrote:

> It is of the loudest Victorian (so-called) Gothic, and a heavy disagreeable mass of building, without skyline or outline of any kind, with huge Brobdignagian sash windows and moulded lintels etc, ten times worse than those of Mr Waterhouse's [New University] Club in St James's Street [London].[126]

Figure 80
Like a smaller sibling of the Granville Hotel, Florence Terrace on Albert Road bears many of the hallmarks of E W Pugin's distinctive style.
[DP251262]

Pugin completed the promenade and bridleway in front of the hotel, while to the east he added a sunken garden, with fountains and an arcade, used as a bowling ground in the summer and flooded in the winter to provide a skating rink. A tunnel was bored through the cliff, leading guests directly down to the beach, while construction was started on an inclined drive or esplanade providing direct access from the Sands to the east cliff. Pugin also contemplated a second hotel against the cliff face, served by a seaside terrace and landing pier, although in the event these remained unrealised.

While much of Pugin's land was sold onto others, he completed a handful of schemes which hint at his vision of St Lawrence-on-Sea. In all probability he was responsible for Florence Terrace (3–13 Albert Road), an ornate group of c 1870 with round turret-like oriels at the corner (Fig 80). Pugin's 1866 purchase also included the narrow strips of land along Lodge Road. Here he built a series of workers' houses and St Augustine's Roman Catholic Elementary School. In December 1866 he renamed the thoroughfare Artillery Road in honour of the Ramsgate Corps of the

Figure 81
The Granville Marina, an inclined promenade linking Ramsgate Sands with the hotels and lodging houses of the east cliff, is featured on this late 19th-century view. The taller, Gothic building was Frederick T Palmer's photographic studio, while the hall at the other end opened as the Établissement. *To the left can be seen the abutment of the railway tunnel opening and the Augusta Stairs, an earlier form of access to the cliff.* [Courtesy of Michael Child]

Cinque Ports Artillery Volunteers which he captained. At a gathering of the Corps to 'christen' the road, the chaplain, the Revd A. Whitehead declared his hope that 'the purchase would be profitable to the captain, and that beautiful villas and terraces would spring up to commemorate the splendid though peaceable victories they had'.[127] As at Mary Townley's 1797 address to the Ramsgate volunteers, profit, patriotism and civic advancement were inseparably linked.

A combination of financial pressure, litigation and overwork brought Pugin's ventures on the east cliff to a premature close and in October 1872 he filed for the liquidation of his estate. The Granville was repossessed by Coutts Bank, to whom Pugin had mortgaged it as security for loans totalling over £100,000.[128] Poignantly, when the Granville Hall, along with a fives court and an 'American bowling alley', was added in 1873–4, it was designed not by Pugin but by John Wimperis of London. In 1876 the hotel and its estate was purchased by the entrepreneur Edmund F Davis, who enclosed the ground in front and completed the inclined drive. Granville Marina, as the latter was known, was overseen by Wimperis and included a parade of shops, tea rooms and houses and an entertainment venue which opened as the *Établissement* (Fig 81).

Davis's commercial success spurred others to invest in the Mount Albion estate. Around 1880 the Broadstairs builder William Harrison started work on

eight grand houses named Granville Terrace, their design derived from Pugin's
hotel with the addition of two storeys of glazed balconies (Fig 82). His clients
were Messrs Sankey, Son and Flint, a firm of solicitors who had been associated
with Pugin's 1867 purchase. In the late 1890s Robert Stacey spent £4,000
converting the first three houses into the Hotel St Cloud, reusing the name of the
first house. Renamed San Clu in 1922, the hotel gradually absorbed the rest of
the terrace, but the western half was destroyed by fire in 1928.

The Ellington, Elms and Dane Park estates

The development of the Ellington estate on the west cliff was a different story.
Ellington Farm was held in the reign of Edward I by John, son of Adrian de
Elinton; its holdings straddled the boundary between the parish of St Lawrence
and the vill of Ramsgate, the formation of which it predated (Figs 83, 84). In 1773
John Garrett acquired a portion of the estate and in the early 19th century

remodelled the farm house, whose grounds in 1893 became Ellington Park. In 1866, the Garrett family trustees auctioned off the estate as building land. The house and grounds were purchased by Edward C Hailes Wilkie, but the remainder was purchased by the British Land Company, which in turn offered the first plots at auction in March 1867. The company was founded in 1856 as the commercial arm of the National Freehold Land Society. Through a modus operandi of subdividing large pieces of land into small building plots for sale, it realised the Society's objective of extending the franchise through property ownership.

A farm track leading from the rope walk (later Cannon Street) to Grange Road became Ellington Road, while Crescent Road ran in a broad sweep to the south. Most of the plots fronted a series of parallel residential roads. End plots

Figure 83
Birds-eye View of Ramsgate, *published in 1861 by H M Ridgway. Holy Trinity Church dominates the partially developed Mount Albion Estate. The as-yet undeveloped Ellington estate can be seen above the spire of Christ Church, while the site of the future Dane Park Estate lies beyond Hereson Road at the top right corner.*
[DP251290; courtesy of Sally and Rob Holden]

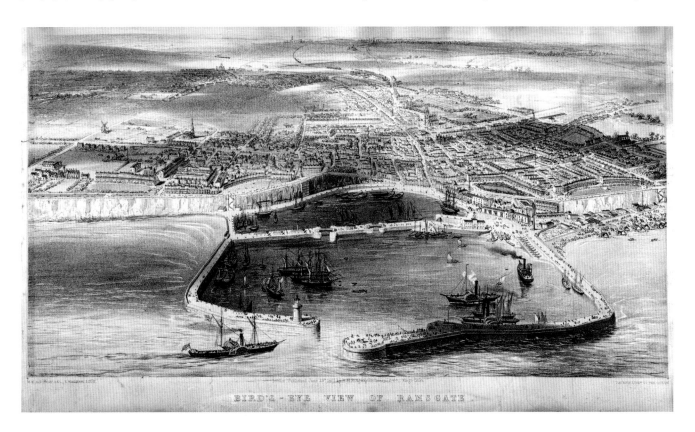

BIRD'S - EYE VIEW OF RAMSGATE.

ST. GEORGE'S CHURCH, RAMSGATE.
TAKEN FROM THE FIELDS NEAR ST LAWRENCE.

Figure 84
This 1830 view by George Sidney Shepherd shows the new church and the upper part of High Street, viewed across the fields of the Ellington estate.
[DP251288; courtesy of Sally and Rob Holden]

presented a design challenge: in order to avoid a blank gable wall, some terraces terminated in a higher-specification 'corner villa', entered from the quieter side street. Lack of coordination between neighbouring developments sometimes resulted in awkward junctions, such as the lack of access between Elms Avenue and Ellington Road before a 20th-century road improvement scheme. The more desirable locations were on the elevated ground towards the top of Ellington Road and South Eastern Road, more likely to offer sea views and away from the smells of the brewery and maltings on Queen Street. Grandest were the detached villas built on wide plots bought up by individual owners who commissioned a bespoke design from a local architect or builder. Some followed a Victorian Gothic style, suggesting the architectural influence of the Pugin family, while others took on a more eclectic appearance.

With limited access to working capital, local house builders operated on a relatively hand-to-mouth basis, building a few pairs of houses at a time and selling them on as soon as they could. The story of Codrington Villas (4–20 Codrington Road) illustrates the perils of property speculation. This terrace of nine houses was developed in 1868–70, ostensibly by Henry Edward Osborn, a builder who was probably acting on behalf of his former employer E W Pugin. Osborn took out a mortgage of £1,000 in his name to finance the project, obtaining designs from Pugin. In 1869 Osborn ran out of money and construction ground to a halt. After the properties were repossessed, the three unfinished houses were purchased by none other than Pugin who obtained an interest-only mortgage to complete them.

As with Ellington, the smaller Elms estate to the south was initiated by an 'outsider', Frederick James Castle of Tunbridge Wells. In 1865 he purchased The Elms, a house built in 1830 by the brewer Richard Tomson, and had it laid out for the erection of 'superior villa residences'.[129] By 1872 several pairs of grand villas were occupied to the north of the site, while Tomson's gardener's cottage was cleared to make way for Marlborough Road.

On a larger scale was the 42-acre Dane Park estate on the fields north-west of Hereson Road, the brainchild of the architect Alfred Robert Pite (1832–1911). As a young man Pite was articled to W G Habershon, with whom in 1860 he established a partnership, with offices in London and Ramsgate. In 1878 he struck out as a sole practitioner, enabling him to focus on Dane Park. He devised a curvilinear layout for the estate, which boasted respectable and recently established neighbours in the form of St Luke's Church and South Eastern College. Pite advertised building plots for sale with peppercorn rents for two years, upon which 'arrangements can be made to erect houses suited to the requirements of any purchaser'.[130] He designed several residences in 'Old English', 'Domestic Gothic' and 'French Chalet' styles, but business proved slow and the remaining plots were sold on to local house builders.[131]

5
20th-century Ramsgate

Entertainment

In 1901 Ramsgate was second only to Folkestone as Kent's largest resort. From the end of the 19th century the town's leaders took a greater interest in preserving Ramsgate's lead by promoting the resort through publicity campaigns, guidebooks and an information bureau. Holiday associations such as the Workers' Travel Organisation, the Holiday Fellowship and the Co-operative Holidays Association organised outings to the seaside for working-class families. By 1939 Ramsgate received a million visitors annually and contemplated extending the holiday season to receive the growing numbers of workers entitled to paid holidays.

The 20th century relaxed the way the seaside was enjoyed. Mixed-sex bathing was cautiously introduced after the First World War and the Borough Council finally ceased licensing bathing machines in 1926. Instead bathers got changed in a licenced 'bathing box' or beach hut, of which 35 were erected at a 1914 bathing platform adjacent to the marina pier.

The Sands, Ramsgate's prime recreational facility, was long hemmed in by shipping, industry and transport interests, namely the pier and its slipways, a masons' yard and the railway station. A shelter, known as the colonnade, had been put up in 1877 to protect visitors from the elements and the eyesore of the stone yard, but 20 years later it was damaged by a storm, affording the opportunity to look afresh at the site. In early 1903 the corporation asked Stanley Davenport Adshead (1868–1947), already engaged on the design of the library, to draw up plans for an entertainment pavilion. 'Perhaps flushed with success I produced a design in a week and was instructed to carry it out in time for the season', he recalled, 'which meant that it had to be completed in six months'.[132] The Royal Victoria Pavilion was duly opened in June 1904 by Princess Louise, Duchess of Argyll (Fig 85).

Although the corporation wanted facilities to impress, they fretted that a two-storey building would bring claims from residents whose sea views had been infringed. Adshead proposed a tall single-storey pavilion with a great central hall whose curved Mansard roof rose above a roof promenade. A pair of flanking wings, octagonal in shape, housed a tea room and buffet, with shop fronts built into a ground-floor colonnade. A domed entrance porch was flanked by figures depicting Art and Song. Inspired by the Royal Opera at Versailles, the

A coloured map drawn by Bernard Willis, an art master at the Thanet School of Art, to commemorate the 50th anniversary of the Borough's incorporation in 1884. In designing the map Willis used aerial photographs taken by Group Captain E R Manning of RAF Manston.
[Courtesy of Michael Child]

Figure 85
A coloured postcard showing the Royal Victoria
Pavilion around the time of its opening in 1904.
[DP251295; courtesy of Sally and Rob Holden]

hall was equipped with a proscenium stage for concerts and variety
performances, but the seating could be cleared for dances and banquets. From
side balconies access could be gained to the roof terrace which encircled the hall.

Asked to provide a shelter for the concerts held at the Italian Gardens, the
borough engineer T G Taylor looked to Margate's recently completed Winter
Gardens (Fig 86). The West Cliff Concert Hall, which opened two days before
the outbreak of hostilities in July 1914, was dug into the cliff so that its flat roof,
supported on iron columns, forms part of the seafront promenade. Highly glazed
walls opened onto a clifftop balcony, while the landward side gave access to a
sunken garden which incorporated ramps for disabled or infirm visitors. A
circular bandstand was centred on the garden elevation so that one half was
inside and the other projected out of the building, an ingenious arrangement
which allowed the audience to be seated *al fresco* in the summer while using the
auditorium during inclement weather.

A variety of visitor attractions came about through private enterprise. After
its closure (page 121), the old terminus at the Sands was in 1930 converted to
Merrie England, a '"closed park" on semi-American lines'.[133] Again Margate
provided a precedent in the form of the Hall by the Sea, later Dreamland, which

Figure 86
The highly glazed interior of the West Cliff Concert Hall around the time of its opening in 1914. The circular stage to the right overlooks a sunken garden, while doors in the opposite wall give access to a sea-facing balcony.
[Courtesy of Phil Spain]

initially occupied the former station booking hall on the seafront. Merrie England was the brainchild of the inventor Granville Bradshaw who initially contemplated recreating an Indian temple along the lines of a display at the British Empire Exhibition, but settled on a nostalgic Old English theme, hiring W Everard Healey to remodel the old station.[134] 'It is a concrete castle, hideous to look at, and full of fun kiosks and inducements to spend pennies', the *Daily Herald* reported.[135] The attraction was overhauled with moderne styling in 1935 by Ramsgate Olympia Ltd, which in 1938 opened the 900-seat Coronation Hall.

Seeking to connect their seafront attractions to the railway network, Ramsgate Olympia in 1936 re-opened part of the redundant line from Ramsgate Sands as a narrow-gauge underground railway. The electric trains of the tunnel railway ran for about 700m before branching off to emerge at a new station at Hereson Road, a short walk from the mainline Dumpton Park station. Aimed at the tourist trade, the World Scenic Railway, as it was called, featured illuminated scenery depicting Switzerland, Canada, the Netherlands, Japan and Egypt.

Between the wars the brewers Tomson and Wotton sought to diversify into operating licenced leisure venues. In 1935 they opened a Marina Bathing Pool and Boating Lake next to Granville Marina. Designed in the Hennebique system

of reinforced concrete by L.G. Mouchel & Partners with the architect
J H Somerset, the facility included an Olympic-sized swimming pool with diving
board and chutes, overlooked by a modernist café with a rooftop car park. To the
east was a boating lake. W J Martin Tomson, the company chairman, was a
patron of modern architecture, commissioning the architect Oliver Hill to design
the Prospect Inn at Minster and an extension for his home at Broadstairs.
Tomson and Wotton also acquired the dance hall and licenced premises at the
Granville Marina, commissioning murals from the artist Rex Whistler. At the
Western Undercliff, meanwhile, the brewers built a paddling pool to accompany
an artificial beach constructed by the borough council.

The interwar period was marked by a renewed enthusiasm for fresh air,
sunlight and outdoor activities, ranging from sunbathing to sanatoria (Fig 87).
Recreation and sports grounds provided 'green lungs' in areas of new suburban
housing. Jacky Baker's Recreation Ground in Northwood opened in 1924 with
football, cricket and hockey pitches. The nine-acre site, named after the farm of
which it was formerly part, was donated to the town by Dame Janet Stancomb-
Wills who later funded a sports pavilion (1927) and tea pavilion (1929) designed
by W Everard Healey.

Figure 87
This painting by the marine artist Charles Pears (1873–
1958) was commissioned in 1935 by the Southern
Railway for use on its promotional posters. The girl in
the foreground holds a small crab.
[Darnley Fine Art]

More glamorous manifestations of the outdoor trend were open-air ballroom dancing and sunbathing. Around the new bandstand which opened at Wellington Crescent Gardens in May 1939 was a surfaced dance floor (Fig 88). Designed in the office of the borough engineer R D Brimmell, the bandstand cost £2,500 and was clad in 'ceramic marble' manufactured by Carter & Co of Poole, Dorset. Brimmell's Eagle Café on the east pier head included two decks of sun terraces. Opening in July 1938, the café was aimed at the passengers of the Eagle and Queen Line Steamers which embarked from the pier. 'Designed to give the appearance of a ship's super-structure', the building is an example of what the artist John Piper termed the nautical style of modern architecture, while its interiors boasted a mural scheme of brightly coloured fish.[136]

Roller skating became a popular, if short-lived pastime from the 1870s, facilitated by the 1865 invention of the 'rocking' skate by J L Plimpton of New York. In 1876 two skating rinks opened at Ramsgate: one was designed by Pugin & Pugin for the Ramsgate Skating Rink Company on a gap site which

Figure 89
The Odeon Cinema at the corner of King Street and
Broad Street, photographed by John Maltby on its
opening in August 1936. Management was taken over
by the Classic Cinemas chain in 1967 but the cinema
closed in 1985.
[BB87/03330]

was later redeveloped as Sanger's Amphitheatre. Another rink, at Pegwell Bay, formed the main attraction of James Tatnell's Ravenscliff Gardens. Edwardian Britain was again gripped by an American-style craze for 'rinking'. Ramsgate's County Rink opened in 1910, part of a speculative boom described by one journalist as 'the skating rinks that mushroom-like / came springing up at morn'.[137] Located on Dumpton Park Drive, the venue was designed by Horace Dan of Faversham for Shoolbred, Moss and Vardon, who also put up rinks at Margate, Chatham and Rochester. It re-opened in 1937 as 'Britain's largest and finest glider skating rink', equipped for rubber-wheeled skates, but after the Second World War was converted into a tool factory and renamed County Works.[138]

Cinemas are amongst the most recognisable of 20th-century building types, but the first moving pictures were shown in theatres or music halls, while early cinemas were often converted from such venues. As early as 1897 St George's Hall hosted 'Lloyd's cinematograph', and the venue re-opened in 1910 as Shanly's Electric Theatre. Ramsgate's earliest purpose-built cinema was probably the King's Cinema of 1910 on King's Place, designed by H. Bertram Langham of Broadstairs for Ramsgate and District Popular Amusements. Its proscenium arch and rear balcony betray a clear debt to theatre design. It was followed by the faïence-clad Ramsgate Picture House, which opened its doors at 59–61 High Street in 1920. In August 1936 the Birmingham-based Odeon chain opened a characteristically moderne cinema on King Street, designed by Andrew Mather (Fig 89). Like many contemporary Odeons it included an adjacent shopping parade (22–30 King Street) which survived the demolition of the cinema in 1988.

Extending the seafront

After the First World War Ramsgate embarked on a programme of seafront improvements to the east and west cliffs, initiated by Ramsgate's first woman mayor, Dame Janet Stancomb-Wills (1854–1932). She asked the distinguished architect Sir John James Burnet (1857–1938) to come up with a scheme that could be executed in phases as funding allowed. Despite being exhibited at the Royal Academy, the project was deferred by the borough council on financial grounds (Fig 90). Undeterred, Dame Janet funded the first portion, Winterstoke Gardens, naming it after her adoptive uncle, Sir William Henry Wills, Baron Winterstoke, whose seaside residence, East Court, she inherited. Burnet's Italianate design was laid out in 1921–3 on an eight-acre site between the Granville Marina and East Cliff Lodge and incorporated formal lawns, terraced rock gardens, a central fountain and a semi-circular sun shelter in the form of a Doric colonnade (Fig 91).

The garden was landscaped by Pulham & Sons, whose Pulhamite rockworks establish continuity with the cliff approach scheme of the 1890s. Despite the involvement of outside specialists, as much use as possible was made of local labour and locally sourced materials to relieve local unemployment. In 1935–6 the corporation devised a scheme to link the gardens with the sea and a new bathing pool via an undercliff drive. The Winterstoke Undercliff took the form of a Pulhamite sea wall into which was let a flight of steps descending the cliff to a concrete promenade reclaimed from the sea. The rockwork was superintended by J W Hitching of J Pulham & Sons who, it was reported, had overseen the

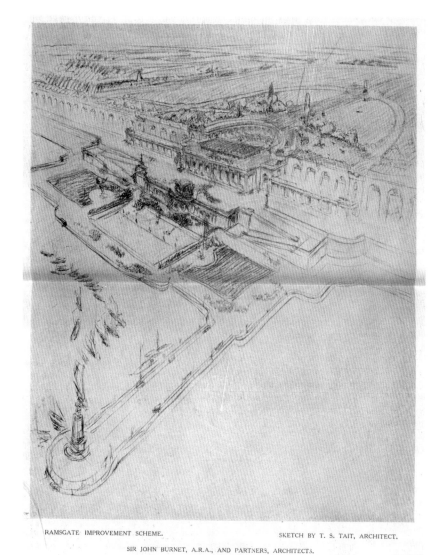

RAMSGATE IMPROVEMENT SCHEME.   SKETCH BY T. S. TAIT, ARCHITECT.

SIR JOHN BURNET, A.R.A., AND PARTNERS, ARCHITECTS.

Figure 90
One of a set of sketch designs produced by Sir John Burnet & Partners c 1920 as part of a seafront improvement proposal. This drawing, by Burnet's partner T S Tait, shows a multilevel entertainment centre on the site of Winterstoke Gardens.
[Royal Academy of Arts, London]

Figure 91
The classical sun shelter at Winterstoke Gardens,
designed by Sir John Burnet & Partners. At the centre of
the colonnade was a fountain incorporating a punning
sculpture by Gilbert Bayes of children playing with a
ram. While this does not survive, Bayes's relief in the
form of a heraldic shield depicting a similar subject can
be seen above.
[DP114435, Peter Williams]

construction of Madeira Walk, Winterstoke Gardens and an earlier chine on the west cliff.[139]

Having in 1921 purchased the Warre estate on the west cliff, the borough council sought a layout. After announcing that they felt unable to proceed with Burnet's master plan, they held a design competition, adjudicated by S D Adshead. In October 1922 the council selected the entry of Franklin & Deacon of Luton, whom Adshead had placed third, on the grounds that it represented the best value for money. Of the 114 acres of purchased land, 30 acres of seafront was set aside as a public recreation ground. In 1923 the remainder was sold off to a house-building syndicate headed by Franklin & Deacon. Their layout, marketed as the St Lawrence Cliffs estate, incorporated two of the corporation's existing schemes: London Road, which opened in 1923, and a sea wall and undercliff drive designed by the borough engineer.

Work commenced in 1924 and in November 1926 the Prince of Wales opened Royal Esplanade, a broad boulevard planted with trees, and Prince Edward Promenade which continued West Cliff Promenade. These defined a long strip laid out in 1928–9 with putting greens, tennis courts, a bowling green and a miniature golf course, provided with shelters and pavilions designed by

Figure 92
A 1932 Aerofilms photograph of the bandstand and pavilions which formed the centrepiece of Prince Edward Promenade on the west cliff. The reinforced-concrete bandstand was demolished in 1961 to make way for a boating pool. Inland are the grounds of Belmont and the largely unbuilt plots of the St Lawrence Cliffs estate.
[EPW039347]

Basil C Deacon (1878–1958). The total cost of about £250,000 was raised by a halfpenny rate, subsidised by a grant from the government's Unemployment Grants Committee in recognition of the corporation's use of direct labour to relieve local unemployment.

At the centre of the roughly symmetrical layout, Deacon designed a circular bandstand 'in the Italian renaissance style' and constructed of reinforced concrete faced with artificial stone (Fig 92).[140] Flanking pavilions defined a sunken central area where deckchairs could be laid out. Contrasting with the formality of the bandstand and pavilions was the picturesque chine or marine gulley, landscaped in Pulhamite rockwork by J Pulham & Sons, which descended to the Western Undercliff. A shortcut to the foreshore was provided by the West Cliff Lift, again designed by Deacon and erected by W W Martin.

Building for the community

By the end of the 19th century it was embarrassingly evident that Ramsgate's motley collection of schools did not add up to an education system. Older children were particularly poorly served and they became the focus of initial reforms. From 1889 local authorities were permitted to levy a penny rate towards providing facilities for vocational or technical instruction, and an Act of 1890 diverted so-called 'whisky money' – the residue of customs and excise duties –to help run them. With a grant of £447 from Kent County Council, Ramsgate took its first steps towards state education. From 1891 'technical classes' in chemistry, shorthand, typewriting, cookery and other subjects were provided in a variety of makeshift venues including the Town Hall and Rock House in Chatham Place. In 1895 a combined public library and technical institute opened at Cavendish House, endowed with a thousand volumes by the philanthropist J Passmore Edwards. When these growing services outgrew the converted building the decision was taken to co-locate them on a single site.

In 1901 the corporation purchased 20 Effingham Street, which came with nearly two acres of land extending back to Elms Avenue. A design competition for a new library and technical institute, assessed by the civic architect Henry Hare, was won by S D Adshead. It was his first commission, although he had established a reputation as a talented perspectivist and as the architectural equivalent of a ghost writer. In his plan, submitted 'at the last moment with the ink wet', the library and school accommodation was ranged around a top-lit central hall, with additional school rooms on the first floor.[141]

But the corporation failed to take into account the 1902 Education Act, under which Kent County Council inherited responsibility for secondary and higher education. This effectively precluded a two-in-one scheme. Instead, a decision was taken to split the site in two. Adshead responded with a scaled-down library in red-orange brick with buff limestone dressings in a classical revival style (Fig 93). It was erected in 1904 with a £7,000 grant by the Scottish American philanthropist Andrew Carnegie. After the interior was gutted by fire in 2004, the library was rebuilt behind the surviving façade.

The remainder of the site was transferred to Kent County Council. The Ramsgate County School was built in 1908–9 for £11,222 to designs by W H Robinson, architect to the Kent Education Committee. For reasons of

Figure 93
An Edwardian photograph of Ramsgate Library, taken
before the garden of Guildford Lawns was developed.
On the left the United Literary Club of 1868 can be seen
in its original form.
[DP251289; courtesy of Sally and Rob Holden]

economic expediency rather than education it was planned as a 'dual school', combining separate facilities for 150 boys and the same number of girls. For the corner site Robinson devised a butterfly plan in which angled wings of the two schools converged on a corner entrance, with a shared assembly hall at the rear. Evening technical classes continued on the first floor. After an educational reorganisation scheme of 1921, the boys' school relocated to Chatham House while the Clarendon Gardens site became Clarendon House County Grammar School for Girls.

The borough council's education committee, meanwhile, became the local education authority for the purpose of elementary education (for children aged between five and eleven). In 1909 a new elementary school was opened on Lillian Road in Hereson, with an infants' school located across the road. Designed in the office of the borough engineer T G Taylor in a neo-Georgian style, its double-decker layout accommodated 380 girls in eight ground-floor classrooms of varying size, and as many boys in a similar configuration on the upper floor. Provision in St Lawrence was expanded with Ellington Girls' School on Ellington Place (1913–4, Graham Tucker). Elementary education was overhauled following the 1926 Hadow report, resulting in the construction of the Dame Janet Junior and Infants' School on Newington Road (1932–3), Ellington Infant School (1938–9) and Hollicondane Senior Boys' School (1939–40), all designed by the borough's school architect, Ernest Barber.

Around the turn of the 20th century it was agreed to replace the old fire station in York Street. After the borough council declined a proposal by the captain of the fire brigade for a new station on St Luke's Recreation Ground, it was decided to convert 20 Effingham Street, which the corporation had acquired with the library and school site in 1901. This double-pile townhouse was remodelled to incorporate two large fire bays, between which was installed a bronze plaque complete with fire bell. A similar strategy was later adopted for Cavendish House, which in 1929–30 was converted into a police station (Fig 94).

After serving the community for half a century, the Seamen's Infirmary was replaced in 1909 by Ramsgate General Hospital on the other side of West Cliff

Figure 94
Ramsgate Police Station on Cavendish Street, adapted in 1929–30 by H H Stroud from the mid-19th-century Cavendish House. In 2019 the site was being redeveloped as a complex of residential apartments.
[DP247224]

Road. Designed by Woodd & Ainslie, the architects to Guy's Hospital in London, the entrance and outpatients' department were housed in a central block with flanking wings each containing a pair of wards. The cost of the new facility was met by a £16,000 legacy from John Nicholas, a retired merchant, while the site was given by Caroline Ashley Murray Smith, granddaughter of J A Warre, the first president of the Infirmary. Later buildings, in a similar neo-Georgian style, included a children's ward (1923–5, W T Stock of Hinds & Son), nurses' home (1926–7) and maternity ward (1931).

Ramsgate's post office was rebuilt in 1908–9 to designs by Henry A Collins of the Office of Works. It replaced a single-storey Gothic Revival structure of 1865, possibly designed by E W Pugin for the town's postmaster, J B Hodgson. The new post office, set back on a new building line, was a confident red-brick and Portland stone building whose Edwardian Baroque idiom complemented that of the new library and hospital.

Early social housing

Ramsgate's tradition of charitable benefaction continued into the 20th century through the endowment of several almshouses for elderly people. Opened in 1899 by the Bishop of Dover, Barber's Almshouses on Elms Avenue was endowed by Frances Barber, a prominent local benefactor, in memory of her late husband and son (Fig 95). Designed by W G Osborne with Langham & Cole, the Elizabethan-style range accommodated 12 elderly persons, ten women and two men, who each received weekly alms of seven shillings. A private chapel is located over the central entrance.

Less well known is Emma Simmons's Almshouses of 1923–4. Simmons, who died in 1912, endowed land on Napleton Road in Southwood on which ten houses were to be built for not more than £850 each. The architect, W T Stock of Hinds & Son, avoided the traditional u-shaped almshouse format in favour of a two-storey terrace, discreetly set back from the road. The result resembles London County Council's early, Arts and Crafts-tinged housing.

After 1918, returning servicemen looking to re-establish households, together with the five-year hiatus in house building, drove an increased need for small houses or cottages. Their number was swollen by miners at Chislet colliery

Figure 95
Barber's Almshouses on Elms Avenue were erected in 1899 by J H Forwalk for a cost of £3,850.
[DP247308]

who took houses in Ramsgate. The so-called Addison Act of 1919 paved the way for the mass provision of municipal housing for rent but in 1921 government subsidies fell victim to the 'Geddes Axe' of economic retrenchment. In 1919 the borough council attempted to build houses on the fields that later formed the site of Dumpton Park station. Land was purchased and designs commissioned from W Everard Healey but progress was halting and in March 1922 the Ministry of Health declined to sanction the scheme.

Ramsgate took immediate advantage of the increased subsidies enacted by the 1924 Housing (Wheatley) Act, and alderman Charles Nixon, chairman of the housing committee, drove through a £191,061 housing scheme at Whitehall Road in the north of the borough. Of the 360 houses, 100 were of the smaller type without a front parlour, whilst the remainder were 'parlour houses'. Planned in the office of the borough surveyor T G Taylor, the layout included Nixon Avenue and Wheatley Road. In 1926 the borough council embarked upon a town planning scheme for the borough with the objective of co-ordinating further expansion and strategic development.

Legislation in the 1930s directed grants towards slum clearance, easing overcrowding and providing 'new houses for old'. From the start the borough council had possessed legal powers to condemn insanitary housing and in 1920 it ordered the demolition of 25 dwellings, mostly small rows of early 19th-century cottages off King Street. In 1930, in response to the new Housing Act, the borough surveyor drew up a five-year programme of slum clearance and 'improvement areas'. Parts of Packers Lane, James Street, Sion Passage, High Street St Lawrence and Newcastle Hill disappeared in clouds of dust and in 1938 it was reported that 'the town looks in places rather like Barcelona after an air raid'.[142]

Many of the displaced residents were rehoused in two- and three-bedroom houses on Bright's Place, a curved road laid out in 1932 on the site of the cleared Ratcliff Square. Nixon's final housing scheme was completed at West Dumpton in 1938, rehousing 100 families from slum clearance areas in Rodney Street, Monkton Place, Bellevue Cottages and Bristol Place. On Ellen Avenue was laid out a distinctive block of flats for older couples, the upper pairs of flats reached via an external flight of stairs (Fig 96).

Smaller houses continued to be built privately between the wars, but for sale, not rent. In 1925 the borough council approved the sale of speculative

Figure 96
Much early council housing was provided with families in mind. Completed in 1938, the borough council's West Dumpton housing scheme included two blocks of eight flats designed for older couples. They are situated on Ellen Avenue, which was named after Ellen Nixon, a former lady mayoress of Ramsgate.
[DP251251]

houses erected by Grummant Bros, a local building contractor which had secured an exchequer subsidy. In response to the need for smaller dwellings, large early 19th-century terraces were subdivided into flats or bedsits. After the First World War a 'flats syndicate' purchased several seafront properties which, as Healey observed, were being given up 'on account of the servant question'.[143] He found that former lodging houses lent themselves well to subdivision, although the process had the potential to degrade the architectural character of the buildings.

Transport

Ramsgate's tourism industry attracted novel forms of transport as well as the upgrading of existing road and rail infrastructure. In the Edwardian era new technologies such as electric trams and cliff lifts were both part of the holiday experience as well as improving access for the infirm and disabled. Such schemes were financially risky and usually brought to fruition by national operators with financial backing, access to engineering expertise and experience in the inevitably complex legal negotiations between local authorities and landowners.

A tram service was operated from 1901 by the Isle of Thanet Tramways and Electric Lighting Company. Although it was aimed at seasonal visitors, the service operated all-year round. Passengers could ride electrically powered carriages from a terminus besides the town station to the seafront between Paragon and Wellington Crescent, with the option of continuing to a loop at Broadstairs via Bellevue Road and the newly laid out Dumpton Park Drive. Several derailments were caused by the steep gradients of Royal Parade and Madeira Walk. The trams were replaced by a bus service in 1937, and the tracks were taken up three years later as part of a wartime drive for scrap metal.

By the end of the 19th century, resorts had started to offer visitors the convenience and technological novelty of funicular railways and vertical cliff lifts. At Ramsgate a marina lift was proposed in 1894 but the idea only took off in 1908 when two lifts were installed by Cliff Lifts Ltd, a subsidiary of R Waygood & Co of London. One survives today, restored and in working order, near the Sands station, at the end of Kent Terrace; the other, at Granville Marina, was demolished in 1970.

Ramsgate's third railway station was opened on 2 July 1926 by Southern Railway, replacing the town and harbour stations (Fig 97). But while the scheme helped to rationalise Thanet's railway network, Ramsgate's new station lay over 1.5km away from the Sands, whereas Margate's was adjacent to the beach. Both stations are early works by the architect E Maxwell Fry (1899–1987), later known as a pioneer of modern architecture, but here still practicing the American-accented Beaux Arts style he learned at the Liverpool School of Architecture.

Another station was located at Dumpton Park, accelerating the development of the open land between Ramsgate and Broadstairs. It served a greyhound racetrack on Hereson Road, a venture of 1928 led by J. Henry Iles, who is better known for developing Margate's Dreamland. Nearby attractions included St Luke's football ground, bowls, croquet and tennis pitches and, from 1936, a miniature railway.

From 1935 Ramsgate had its own airport, located at Hope's Lane at Northwood (Fig 98). One of several civil aerodromes operated by the Straight Corporation Ltd, it served private planes, a flying school and a commercial service to Belgium. Designed by David Pleydell-Bouverie, the terminal building

Figure 97 (above)
Ramsgate station of 1924–6 was part of a long–intended scheme by Southern Railway to link the two railway lines at Ramsgate.
[DP247119]

Figure 98 (left)
In Dell & Wainwright's artfully composed photograph of 1937, the streamlined terminal building of Ramsgate Airport is juxtaposed against a Short Scion II cantilever monoplane.
[Dell & Wainwright / RIBA Collections]

was built in 1936–7. Its streamlined, reinforced-concrete structure resembled an aeroplane's wings when viewed from the air, a surprisingly rare evocation of flight in 1930s terminal designs. Fast-developing aeronautical technology demanded flexibility, so all walls were designed as non-load bearing, while the folding and sliding glass and teak doors to the flying club restaurant could be flung open to a paved terrace. Ramsgate Airport closed in 1968 and was later redeveloped as the Pyson's Road Industrial Estate.

Ramsgate at war

Due to its proximity to mainland Europe, Ramsgate was one of Britain's most heavily attacked towns during the First World War. It suffered not only shelling from German destroyers but a new form of attack: air raids from airships and early forms of bombers. Ramsgate's first experience of total warfare came a fortnight before the first raids on London. In the early morning of 17 May 1915 a single Zeppelin airship, flying at a high altitude, dropped about two dozen bombs. Several properties were damaged including the Bull and George Inn where two people died from their injuries. On another occasion an ammunition dump at the harbour was hit, igniting with a blaze which could be seen from Calais. There were deadly accidents too: on 26 May 1917, a torpedo was accidently discharged aboard a torpedo boat while it was moored at the harbour, killing 14 men and causing substantial damage.

Means of air raid warning, shelter and emergency response had to be hastily improvised, while emergency plans were drawn up for the evacuation of the civilian population in the event of invasion. In October 1915, the town's firefighting capabilities were improved when Dame Janet Stancomb-Wills presented the town with its first motorised fire engine, named after Lord Winterstoke. Some residents moved inland while others took shelter in cellars or underground tunnels. In response to the ferocity of the air raids of 1917, over 30 public 'dug-outs' were excavated, most of them located near schools or residential areas. According to a contemporary account, 'people accustomed themselves to spend the night underground, where prayer meetings, concerts and amusements took place'.[144] One shelter, rediscovered when Ellington Girls' School at Ellington Place was redeveloped, consisted of a circuit of tunnels, lined with wooden benches and equipped with separate entrances and zones for boys, girls and infants.[145]

Ramsgate harbour retained its strategic importance, serving from 1913 as the base for the Downs Boarding Flotilla, later absorbed into the Dover Patrol. Its principal tasks included patrolling the Downs and examining the cargoes of merchant vessels for contraband and enemy agents. The harbour area was brought under Admiralty control and closed to the public, with approaches to the harbour and Sands blocked by entanglements of barbed wire. A machine-gun emplacement and searchlights were mounted on Jacob's Ladder, while six armed drifters were moored in the inner basin.

The First World War marked the beginning of military aviation. In May 1916 a Royal Naval Air Station was established in the open fields at Manston, about 5km east of Ramsgate, replacing a seaplane landing ground at Westgate. Its earliest buildings, a series of timber huts, were soon joined by two sub-surface hangars, a railway line to Birchington, a power generator and barracks. After the war Manston remained operational and an RAF school of technical training was established there. During the First World War acoustic technology was developed to provide advance warning of incoming hostile aircraft, particularly at night. One of the earliest sound mirrors, taking the form of a shallow concrete dish, was installed at Joss Gap at the North Foreland near the end of the war.

Medical and convalescent facilities were in urgent demand for returning service personnel. The Royal Sailors' Rest was taken over as a military hospital by the local branch of the Voluntary Aid Detachment, a unit of trained nurses. In October 1914 it received 53 wounded Belgian soldiers, conveyed to England by the Wounded Allies' Relief Committee. The manor house of Nethercourt, the Granville Hotel, St Lawrence College, Chatham House School and Townley Castle School were among the premises requisitioned for the treatment and recuperation of almost 2,000 wounded Canadian soldiers.

Wartime shortages of skilled labour and materials had a devastating effect on Ramsgate's home front. Inconvenienced by minefields and the absence of the lightships anchored near the Goodwin Sands, its fishing fleet shrank from about 200 boats employing 800 men to no more than a dozen small boats, each with a crew of two. In response to food shortages caused by U-boat attacks on merchant shipping, the town's recreation grounds and patches of waste ground were cleared to create over 200 'war allotments'. A Ramsgate 'national kitchen' was established at Queen Street in May 1918, following the recommendations of the Ministry of Food by providing inexpensive meals at a set price.

By the end of the war, the town had been targeted by 396 bombs and 343 shells, killing a total of 45 people and injuring 93. Most of the 102 men and women of the Commonwealth forces buried at Ramsgate Cemetery served in the army or navy, with a smaller number of Royal Flying Corps and merchant navy personnel. Ramsgate's war dead, including civilians, are commemorated at the war memorial outside the west door of St George's Church which was dedicated by the Archbishop of Canterbury in October 1920. Designed by Sir Herbert Baker, it takes the form of a tall stone cross on which is carved a three-masted man-of-war, symbolising the town's maritime origins and, on the rear, a figure of St George and the Dragon.

Elsewhere the conflict was marked in different ways. Dame Janet commissioned a memorial from the sculptor Gilbert Bayes. Unveiled at Albion Place Gardens in 1920, 'Destiny' depicts a seated female figure, her face unveiled but her eyes closed (Fig 99). Ex-servicemen raised £1,250 towards a memorial children's ward at the General Hospital, while in 1926–7 a chapel and library, designed by Sir Aston Webb, was added to St Lawrence College in the memory of former pupils who died on active service.

A decade on from the opening of Webb's chapel, preparations were underway for another global conflict. After 1935, in response to Nazi rearmament and aggression, the armed forces and civil defence capabilities were again stepped up. In January 1938 the Air Raid Precautions (ARP) Act came into force, obliging local authorities to prepare ARP schemes. Ramsgate's response, designed by the borough engineer R D Brimmell, was a network of deep tunnel shelters which incorporated the existing railway tunnels on the east cliff. Work commenced immediately after Home Office approval was received in March 1939 and was completed by the Francois Cementation Company of Doncaster at the remarkably low cost of £54,000.

Over 4.5km of tunnels were arranged in a semi-circular circuit beneath Addington Street and Marlborough Road, then north-east to Boundary Road and Victoria Parade where it linked up with the railway tunnel. Spur branches served the General Hospital, Ellington Park and other residential locations. An

Figure 99
Destiny, *a war memorial by Gilbert Bayes, was presented to the town in 1920 by Dame Janet Stancomb-Wills.*
[DP247315]

average of 18m deep, the tunnels were equipped with air vents, drainage, air locks and recesses for toilets and first aid posts. Seating was provided for 35,000, the town's entire population (Fig 100). Twenty-three entrances were distributed so that most residents were no more than five minutes away from shelter, situated in open spaces to minimise the risk of overcrowding. The tunnel network was designed to be capable of post-war conversion to a main sewer system. More remote locations were served by the air raid shelters of 1917–18 and the caves underneath St Augustine's Church and the Granville Hotel, while cut-and-cover trench shelters and steel Anderson shelters were also deployed.

Ramsgate's ARP scheme required a range of facilities. Brimmell's responsibilities also included the erection of 10 reinforced air raid wardens' posts in September 1939. Elsewhere, existing buildings were converted for ARP purposes wherever possible, with the police station reinforced as a control centre and cleansing station, and Prior Road and Ellington infants' schools equipped as first aid posts. An emergency water supply tank was installed at Spencer Square

Figure 100
A Ramsgate family 'at home' in the town's deep tunnel shelters.
[Courtesy of Phil Spain / Ramsgate Tunnels]

Gardens and fire watchers' and ARP wardens' lookout posts were established on the flat roofs of factories and commercial premises (Fig 101).

By early 1940 the prospect of the fall of France and the occupation of the Channel ports made the threat of enemy invasion loom large. Ramsgate again found itself in the first line of defence: unbeknownst to the British Army, the German invasion plans, codenamed Operation Sealion, involved opening up a broad front from Ramsgate to the Isle of Wight, reaching the former from Dunkirk and Ostend. In May the Secretary of State for War Anthony Eden called on men between the ages of 17 and 65 and not in military service to defend their country against invasion by enrolling in the Local Defence Volunteers, later renamed the Home Guard. Ramsgate's citizens responded as readily as had their forebears in the days of the voluntary militias, with 900 volunteers enlisting in the first fortnight, although of these only 400 were classed as 'effective'.[146] In the first week of June 3,386 children – three-quarters of the school population – were evacuated inland, while secret plans were drawn up for the mass evacuation of Ramsgate residents to Guildford, Malden and Surbiton in the event of an enemy landing.

From May 1940, a 'coastal crust' of anti-invasion defences was formed along the British coastline, especially the exposed south and east coasts, with anti-tank 'stop lines' of pillboxes, road blocks and slit trenches further inland. Emergency coastal batteries, some armed with naval guns, were established at Wellington Crescent Gardens, RAF Manston, Chilton, Haine, Northwood, Cliffsend and Dumpton to defend the harbour. The pillboxes defending the harbour were disguised to resemble refreshment huts and ticket kiosks. Entanglements of barbed wire, anti-tank blocks and 'Admiralty scaffolding' were planted at the potential landing sites of Pegwell Bay and the Sands, and sections of the inclined drive to the Western Undercliff were dynamited. Open fields were rigged with anti-glider obstructions including overhead wires strung between posts. The town's appearance was further altered by the removal in August 1940 of over 2.5km of railings from the town's public gardens and open spaces for scrap iron.

In spring 1941, an early form of radar station was installed at the Warre recreation ground off London Road to detect approaching ships and aircraft. Known as the Chain Home Low (CHL) system, it was part of a coastal network which detected low-flying incoming aircraft. Few traces of the coastal defences survive today: a concrete 4in (10cm) gun emplacement stands at Little Cliffsend Farm, as does a group of anti-landing defences at Pegwell Bay, comprising around 60 anti-tank pimples ('dragon's teeth'), 300 anti-tank cylinders and a pillbox.

Ramsgate harbour served as an assembly point for the convoys of small, largely civilian craft despatched to evacuate the British Expeditionary Force from the beaches and harbour of Dunkirk between 26 May and 4 June 1940. In the eyes of one participant, 'the whole course from Ramsgate was like a main street in a busy town, traffic several abreast going each way'.[147] At Ramsgate harbour the 'little ships' were refuelled, repaired and crews allocated, while medical aid and refreshments were provided for the returning troops. The episode is commemorated by a stained glass window in St George's Church, of 1961 by A E Buss.

RAF Manston played a significant role during the Second World War as a forward base for offensive strikes and for the interception of incoming bombers. Such was its strategic importance that it was repeatedly bombed during the Battle of Britain. It was later developed as a refuelling point and emergency

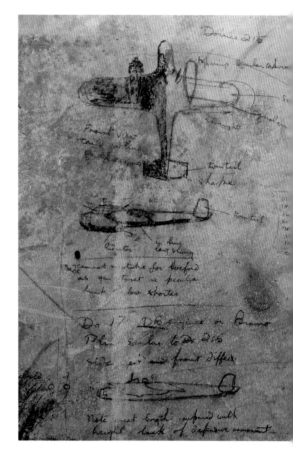

Figure 101
Wartime graffiti on the stairway leading to the flat roof of the former Woolworth's store (12–14 High Street), which may have served as a Royal Observer Corps lookout post. These pencil drawings were made to aid the identification of enemy aircraft, in this case the Dornier Do 215 (top) and Do 17.
[DP247281]

landing ground for bomber crews with the construction in 1943 of a single, wide concrete runway, 3.6km in length. The following year the runway was equipped with the FIDO (Fog Investigation and Dispersal Operation) landing aid in which fog was dispersed by strips of burner jets.

From July 1940 until the V-1 raids of summer 1944, Ramsgate was attacked from the air. The harbour, RAF Manston and the gasworks were amongst the strategic targets, but the raids were often indiscriminate, with returning bombers dumping their payloads on reaching the coast. This was the case on 24 August 1940 when, unable to attack London, German bombers unloaded over 500 high explosive bombs on the town. From February 1941 Ramsgate was shelled by long-range guns until the recapture of the Channel ports by allied forces in summer 1944. In all, 84 civilians were killed or died of their injuries and 262 were injured. Architectural losses included St Mary's Church at Chapel Place, the Methodist Chapel at Hardres Street, St Paul's Church and parts of Albion Place, Sion Hill and the Granville Hotel.

Post-war: redevelopment, preservation, decline

After the war, attention turned to reconstruction and the rejuvenation of the tourist economy after six years of neglect. Visitor restrictions were lifted, the bomb-damaged Granville Marina and Marina bathing pool were restored, coastal defences were cleared away and the town's hotels and boarding houses were put in order. Like other seaside resorts, Ramsgate was predominately seeking to restart its tourism industry where it had left off in 1939, though where there had been losses, some of these were replaced. The Foy Boat Hotel and neighbouring properties were rebuilt in a sympathetic if somewhat old-fashioned manner. After the concert pavilion on Victoria Parade was deemed to be beyond repair it was replaced in 1946–7 with the Granville Theatre, designed by the new borough architect W W Garwood. With the exception of the fly tower, its height was capped at 2.7m in height due to restrictive covenants preserving the sea views of neighbouring properties.

During the first decades of the 20th century, a growing number of people enjoyed disposable income and increasing amounts of paid and unpaid leave.

Figure 102
H R Steele's 1944 scheme for a holiday health centre on the grounds of East Cliff Lodge.
[The Builder]

This culminated in 1938 with the Holidays with Pay Act, which began to focus concern on how resorts would manage an even larger numbers of holidaymakers.[148] This led commentators to fear that largely unspoilt stretches of coastline previously fairly immune from the tourist gaze would begin to succumb to new developments as a result of a combination of new transport and the increased right to a holiday. Holiday camps, the earliest of which appeared in England in the early 20th century, were felt to be one solution to the problem, particularly since the huge camps created by Billy Butlin from 1936 onwards seemed to offer the answer to the pent-up demand expected to be released from 1945 onwards.

The borough council entertained several proposals for a permanent holiday camp and allocated a site in its 1943 town planning scheme but the idea was quashed by local opposition and concern over 'competition with the landladies of the town'.[149] In 1944 the architect Harold Rooksby Steele concocted a visionary design for a holiday health centre on the East Cliff Lodge estate, which had been sold off in 1935 (Fig 102). Visitors would experience 'the atmosphere of a sea cruise' with six streamlined 'land-ships', each accommodating 216 guests.[150] Covered ways gave access to a central recreation block with an 800-seat restaurant, concert hall, cinema, gym and ballroom-cum-ice rink. After this and other proposals failed to materialise, the borough council compulsorily purchased the estate in 1950. East Cliff Lodge was demolished in July 1953 and its grounds became the King George VI Memorial Park.

In the stringent austerity economy, new attractions tended to be relatively modest, making use of existing sites. The 1951 Festival of Britain was marked with a 'festival of light' in which over 3km of seafront were lit up with special displays. Concrete fountains illuminated with coloured lights were installed in the inner basin of the harbour, Nelson Crescent Gardens and Victoria Gardens, of which the last survives (Fig 103). Deliberately miniature in scale was Castlewode, Ramsgate's model village which opened in 1953 in the grounds of West Cliff Lodge. The creation of the model maker Jack Scott of Westgate, it included half-timbered houses, a winding stream, a battlemented castle and a

Figure 103
Although centred on London's South Bank, the 1951 Festival of Britain was a national celebration with exhibitions and associated events across the country. This fountain at Victoria Parade, originally illuminated with coloured lights, formed part of Ramsgate's contribution, dubbed a 'festival of light'.
[DP251105]

131

modern airport. The artificial beach at the Western Undercliff was renewed and a three-storey, reinforced-concrete block of chalets was built there in 1961.

Ramsgate's housing needs were discussed as early as February 1943, when it was anticipated that returning members of the armed forces would demand homes in which to start new families and households. The town had lost 373 buildings, most of them dwellings, to enemy action, with a further 340 classed as seriously damaged. Having received 500 applications for council houses, in late 1945 the borough council gained ministerial approval for a small development of semi-detached houses adjoining the Jewish cemetery at Hollicondane. They were designed by the newly arrived borough architect Walter Garwood, who brought 'a fund of bright ideas' from previous posts at the London boroughs of Poplar and St Marylebone.[151] Garwood's house plans were compact and efficient, with an open-plan living/dining room and a kitchen equipped with built-in units and a serving hatch. Each semi-detached pair were rotated at a slight angle to the next to avoid a monotonous layout. These first post-war houses were supplemented by 150 prefabricated homes, erected in 1945–6 at Whitehall and Newington as part of a national £150m programme. Of Uni-Seco type, they were manufactured by the Selection Engineering Company Ltd and erected by London contractors.

More ambitious in scale was the 112-acre Newington estate north-east of St Lawrence on which were built 1,060 dwellings. Here Garwood devised an axial layout with streets of semi-detached houses forming two wing-shaped zones flanking a broad central axis. Originally Durban Avenue, the latter was renamed Princess Margaret Avenue in honour of the royal who declared it open in May 1950. Shops, community buildings and the Flowing Bowl pub (designed by R W Stoddart) fringed a central roundabout. At the top of the avenue but deliberately placed off the main axis was St Christopher's, a modest church of plum-coloured brick designed by the Brighton-based practice Denman & Son. A playing field and playground were sited at the south end of the estate, within reach of large infants and junior schools of 1950. Designed by Howard Lobb for Kent County Council, these comprised linear 'fingers' of classrooms joined by corridors.

Ramsgate publicised a zealous development plan in January 1964 prepared by the borough engineer H Spenceley Hole. To be implemented in phases over 15 years, it included a one-way ring road, the pedestrianisation of Harbour Street and the lower part of High Street and seven development areas, some earmarked for slum clearance in the 1930s. The initial stage included the clearance of the area around Leopold Street, a patchwork of early houses, pubs, fish smoking sheds and a Baptist chapel, to allow the construction of a multi-storey car park and shopping precinct: the Argyle Centre, completed in 1975. Political pressure to provide council housing remained acute throughout the 1960s and early 1970s. Three 15-storey towers (Staner Court in Manston Road, and Kennedy House and Trove Court in the Newcastle Hill clearance area) went up in the election year of 1964 using Wimpey's 'no fines' method of concrete construction.

From the late 1960s the Greater London Council (GLC) was active in Thanet, buying up seaside bungalows and flats to let to retired Londoners to free up inner-city sites. Concerns were voiced that this compounded the area's ageing population and placed an additional burden on social care services. The matter came to a head when the GLC purchased a clearance site on the corner of Hardres Street and Brunswick Street on which it planned Brunswick Court, a seven-storey block of 42 flats with an attached community hall. In 1975 Ramsgate's housing authority (by then Thanet District Council [TDC], formed in 1974 as a result of local government reorganisation) exercised an option to buy back the undeveloped site and completed the scheme to rehouse Ramsgate residents. Later housing, overseen by TDC's architect Roman Mirkowski, was low-rise and gentler in appearance: Conflans Court (1978–81) at Camden Square echoes the arched balconies of the early 19th-century Camden Place.

Ramsgate lost a significant proportion of its architectural heritage during the post-war years. Houses set within large plots, such as Nethercourt and Southwood House, were redeveloped as housing, while Townley Castle and Conynham House were absorbed into the respective sites of Chatham House School and Thanet Technical College (Fig 104). The Tomson and Wotton Brewery in Queen Street was bought by Whitbread in 1968 and was promptly closed and redeveloped. Past loss and present threat spurred a group of residents to found the Ramsgate Society in July 1964 with the aim of preserving the town's architectural heritage. One of its initial campaigns was to save Townley House, whose owners applied to demolish the listed building for redevelopment. In 1966 the house was acquired by J C Farley Ltd, a long-established furniture store, for use as a showroom. Many early buildings, such as Queen's Court and the early 18th-century Monkton House (124 High Street) were restored by the

Canterbury conservation architect Anthony Swaine (1913–2013).

The harbour maintained its viability by increasingly focusing on small leisure craft and developing new cross-channel facilities. In April 1966 the Swedish firm Hoverlloyd commenced a crossing to Calais, launching *Swift* and *Sure*, two 38-seat Westgate SR.N6 craft from a radial slipway built against the cross wall. The introduction in 1969 of the larger SR.N4, which carried 250 passengers with 30 cars, saw operations move to a purpose-built hoverport at Pegwell Bay, designed by Barnard, Morris, Evans & Partners. Floating pontoons with berths for over 100 yachts were installed in Ramsgate harbour in 1965. This was a prelude to the conversion of the inner harbour to a 400-berth marina in 1976, with commercial traffic and the lifeboat service continuing to use the outer harbour. The marina stimulated development around the harbour area such as the overscaled Marina Resort Hotel of 1988, although a £90 million mixed-use proposal of 1987–8 by the Dutch developers VOM stalled after local opposition.

Another embarkation point took the form of the West Rocks Ferry Terminal (today known as the Port of Ramsgate), which was constructed in 1979–80 with

Figure 104
The sports hall to Chatham House School is one of Ramsgate's most distinctive pieces of postwar design. Completed in 1962 to designs by Kent County Council's architect's department, it occupies the former site of Townley Castle.
[DP24757]

the reclamation of 18 acres of foreshore adjoining the west pier. A further extension of 1983–4, part-funded by TDC, provided three berths, passenger and wharfage facilities and a detached breakwater which permitted all-weather operations (Fig 105). The facility was managed by a subsidiary of Sally Lines, the Finnish operator which plied a roll-on/roll-off passenger and freight service between Ramsgate and Dunkirk between 1981 and 1998. The chalet block at the

Figure 105
This 2010 Aerofilms photograph, taken from the south-west, shows the late 20th-century ferry terminal. Passenger services ceased in 2013 and the future of the port facility is currently uncertain.
[EAW96658]

Western Undercliff made way for an access road and tunnel, opened in 2000.

For the tourism industry, the decades after the Second World War maintained the offer available during the interwar years. In hindsight, the scale of the challenges it would face were emerging during the 1960s, but despite growing foreign competition the peak of domestic holidays seems to have occurred in the early 1970s. From the mid-1970s onwards, tourism to foreign destinations increased rapidly; in 1978, nine million holidays of four nights or more were taken abroad but nine years later this had risen to 20 million.[152] Foreign destinations initially appealed to a young, more affluent market; a holiday survey commissioned in 1969 by the borough council found that the resort predominantly attracted older visitors with lower than average incomes, many of whom returned every year and were prepared to overlook any decline in standards. Recommendations to attract new generations of holidaymakers included promoting the resort to European tourists, harnessing its architectural and cultural heritage and providing a multi-purpose entertainment centre capable of attracting the lucrative conference trade.[153]

Perceptions of economic decline and mismanagement were exacerbated by the demise of many of the resort's most popular venues, including the Marina Bathing Pool (which closed in 1975 amid fears of structural faults), the former *Établissement* at Marina Parade (latterly Nero's Nightclub, which was demolished in 1996), and Merrie England, latterly Pleasurama, which was gutted by fire in May 1998. Their prominent seafront sites have lain empty ever since, undermining the town's self-image. In addition, the Royal Palace Theatre (formerly Sanger's Amphitheatre) in the High Street was demolished in 1961, as was the theatre at the Granville Hotel in 1982 (despite it being listed). Then undervalued, these are exactly the types of sites that have become highly prized in recent years and might have played an active role in future regeneration schemes.

Ramsgate's rich stock of Georgian and Regency houses was degraded by subdivision of houses into flats or bedsits, creating houses in multiple occupation (HMO). Economic diversity narrowed with the attrition of light industry and marine engineering, while the regional economy was also affected by the closure of the collieries at Chislet, Snowdown, Tilmanstone and Betteshanger. This reduced local job opportunities, already affected by the seasonal and casual nature of the seaside labour economy. Despite a succession of late 20th-century regeneration initiatives, the town's retail trade suffered from dwindling investment, signalled by the closure of the town's branch of Marks and Spencer in 1991.

As the 20th century came to a close, the town faced a series of problems, some of its own making, but most due to national trends away from the traditional British seaside holiday. However, Ramsgate, like other historic seaside resorts, has a long back story and a rich architectural heritage. While this important resource continues to face significant challenges, it will also be key to the regeneration and sustainable development of the town during the 21st century.

> Seaside towns must be inspired to regain their pioneering spirit and evolve to meet present day and future challenges
>
> House of Lords Select Committee report on *The Future of Seaside Towns*[154]

6

Ramsgate's future

The decision to create a Heritage Action Zone in Ramsgate in 2017 recognised the challenges that the town faced, but it was also an affirmation of the strong historical foundations and rich natural resources that could underpin its future prosperity. While Ramsgate has a unique character, there are many issues that it shares with other seaside resorts. One contributor to the House of Lords Select Committee report *The Future of Seaside Towns*, which was published in 2019, stated that the 'seaside towns that have seen the most success in shaking off their negative image … are those that have identified their own special character and unique selling points'.[155] By extension it could be argued that the distinctiveness and historic character of seaside resorts has a central role to play in their regeneration.

Challenges

Seaside resorts once enjoyed a near monopoly of British popular tourism, as the shape of the railway network directed people towards well-connected destinations. However, during the second half of the 20th century a combination of the growth of car ownership, years of underinvestment in accommodation and facilities, increased disposable income and affordable package holidays abroad drew people away from Britain's coast. By the 1960s our seaside resorts were being unfavourably, and sometimes unfairly, compared with bright, new and sometimes incomplete Mediterranean resorts. In addition, resorts have faced greater competition for a family's disposable income from leisure activities that could be reached from home, ranging from visits to theme parks and sporting events to pop festivals and trips to heritage sites.

With such a range of options available, the negative public image that became associated with Britain's seaside resorts acted as a deterrent to many families. Newspaper headlines trumpeted violent seafront clashes between mods and rockers in the 1960s and followed this up with scare stories about benefits claimants, drug hostels and rampant homelessness.

The conversion of the inner basin to a 400-berth marina has brought new life to Ramsgate's Royal Harbour. [Thanet District Council]

Figure 106
Gap sites and derelict buildings detract from the
character and appearance of historic towns and
present an opportunity for high quality and
sympathetic development.
[DP247221]

Unfortunately, behind the headlines lie some hard truths. Seaside communities face significant social and economic problems, including high numbers of people with low skills and a higher than average crime rate. Due to the nature of the tourism sector, workers predominantly earn relatively low wages and their limited spending power is exacerbated by the seasonal and casual nature of their employment. The lack of investment in a seaside resort's economy is reflected on the ground in lingering gap sites, poorly maintained facilities and the subdivision of houses into unsuitable bedsits, creating houses in multiple occupation (HMO) (Fig 106). A vicious circle is evident at some resorts in which declining visitor numbers has led to less private and public investment, leading to underoccupied and low-quality accommodation, the closure of entertainment facilities and, inevitably, fewer visitors.

At the same time, seaside resorts are a magnet for large numbers of affluent people who wish to retire there, leading to the development of contrasting zones of poverty and prosperity. Large numbers of retired people also have an impact on the shape and size of council spending. More money is required to provide the social services that they need and when this is combined with the higher

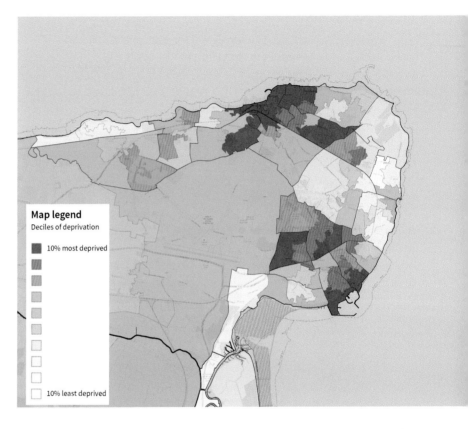

Figure 107
This map illustrates relative deprivation in small areas in Thanet in 2019. The Index of Multiple Deprivation ranks every small area in England from 1 (most deprived area) to 32,844 (least deprived area). The areas coloured dark blue fall amongst the 10 per cent most deprived small areas in England, while the areas coloured white are amongst the 10 per cent least deprived small areas in England.
[Map data © OpenStreetMap contributors]

Map legend
Deciles of deprivation

10% most deprived

10% least deprived

expenditure required to service the facilities that visitors expect, it creates further financial pressures in addition to those faced by all local authorities.

The condition of historic buildings in the centres of resorts is often a direct reflection of the underlying social and economic problems that these towns face. A more statistical picture can be gleaned from interrogating the government's Indices of Multiple Deprivation, a survey carried out every few years.[156] This consistently reveals that seaside resorts feature among the most deprived places in England; of 317 local authority districts in 2019, Blackpool ranked 1st, Hastings 13th and Great Yarmouth 24th. Thanet, which includes Ramsgate and Margate as well as more prosperous resorts and residential areas, was placed 34th.

When the more detailed figures for smaller geographical areas (the so-called lower layer super output areas) are examined, the picture of deprivation and inequality in Ramsgate appears more polarised (Fig 107). In Ramsgate, the areas corresponding to the central core of the town, including most of the seafront, are among the 10 per cent most deprived in England. Areas within Newington and Northwood wards to the north-west feature in the same category, but parts of Nethercourt, Pegwell and Cliffsend wards to the west, along with the areas around Broadstairs to the north-east, are among the least deprived in England.

At the beginning of 2019, 10 per cent of shops in Britain's high streets stood empty.[157] Seaside resorts are prone to relatively high vacancy rates, particularly during the winter months before new businesses refurbish and open for the summer season. A survey carried out in 2018 showed that 16.3 per cent of the shops on Ramsgate's high street were unoccupied, while its equivalent in Margate had a vacancy rate of 26.5 per cent.[158] Both resorts have acutely felt the commercial challenges resulting from the marked shift to online retailing and the impact of out-of-town shopping centres, particularly the Westwood Cross Shopping Centre, which opened in 2005 in the heart of Thanet. Ramsgate's economic resilience has also been impacted by the loss of local industry and changes in farming practice and in the commercial fishing industry.

Many of Ramsgate's current problems arise from its history as a seaside resort, but it has also had to deal with some loss of identity and autonomy. As a result of local government reorganisation in 1974 the town was incorporated into the newly created Thanet District Council, with the result that it has had to compete as well as cooperate with nearby Margate and Broadstairs for investment and profile. A lack of consensus in relation to key development and infrastructure sites has hampered progress, particularly the continuing uncertainty over the future of the Port of Ramsgate, Manston Airport and the Pleasurama site (the former Ramsgate Sands railway station).

Opportunities

Underpinning any growth in tourism must be the need to communicate that Ramsgate is a good place to live, a good place to invest and therefore a good place to visit. But how can Ramsgate's seaside economy, built around the

Figure 108
Gruff Rhys performing at Ramsgate Music Hall in summer 2018. Since opening its doors in 2013, this small live music venue has become part of the town's thriving cultural scene.
[Courtesy of Dik Ng]

traditional summer holiday, reinvent itself to meet the expectations and preferences of 21st-century holidaymakers? Today, a family is more likely to visit Ramsgate for a day trip, a short break or a long weekend than spend a long summer holiday there. Successful resorts tend to be those that provide a quality hub for exploring neighbouring resorts and nearby attractions. As well as being a destination in its own right, Ramsgate is well placed for discovering Kent's coastline, including Whitstable, Herne Bay, Margate, Broadstairs, Sandwich Bay and Deal as well as inland attractions that include Canterbury. A stronger hospitality and food offer would encourage more people to use Ramsgate as a base for excursions into the surrounding area.

While the traditional two-week seaside beach family holiday may still be alive and well, but living on the Mediterranean, this does not mean that England's traditional seaside resorts should abandon this dimension of their history and character. There is still a great appetite for a day out at the seaside and Ramsgate is particularly well placed to exploit it since the opening of the high-speed railway line from St Pancras. Londoners, Britain's largest single market, need to become more aware of the charms awaiting them on the Kent coast, and to this end, the railway operator Southeastern actively promotes cheap summer tickets, allowing holidaymakers to reach Ramsgate in just over an hour.

But seaside towns don't just need to be good places to visit; they need to be good places to live, study and work, with a sufficiently broad-based economy to create services, jobs and opportunities for local people. While its resort heritage is an important element of its make-up, Ramsgate has always been more than a holiday destination. Its improved connectivity and attractive housing stock have the potential to attract inward investment and new residents, particularly young families and a growing creative community (Fig 108).

If Ramsgate is to build on its innate strengths, then chief amongst these is its magnificent harbour. Enclosing 19ha of water, it includes the Royal Harbour Marina, which opened in 1976 and now offers 700 moorings for pleasure craft. While it might not always have the sunshine of the Mediterranean, the harbour has the same liveliness and colour as more exotic ports, and it offers an obvious focus for heritage-led development. Increasing public access and improving the connection between the town and the harbour could stimulate Ramsgate's economic development. There is much scope to celebrate Ramsgate's long relationship with the sea, with its stories of fishing, daring rescues and heroism. The unique but underused Smack Boys' Home on the harbour quayside might be converted into a hotel and restaurant, conveying another aspect of the harbour's extraordinary story. Historic ships might be encouraged to dock at Ramsgate, since they serve to spark the imagination and cast light on the town's colourful maritime history.

Ramsgate needs a bold and imaginative approach to its future. Post-war clearance in York Street and Leopold Street, adjoining the harbour and once the site of Ramsgate's earliest settlement, led to unsympathetic and overscaled developments with blank elevations and unscreened service yards. The regeneration of this area might include a new public square with wide views of the harbour, the sea and ships, improving the connections between the town and its harbour. This new open space might include a maritime museum telling the story of Ramsgate, the North Foreland and the Goodwin Sands.

A few recent developments are notable for having enhanced Ramsgate's historic character and appearance, rather than undermining it. The redevelopment of the former Ramsgate Hospital site, which combines the conversion of listed buildings with low-rise housing, has created a fine-grained residential community. An infill development of ten houses on a Second World War bomb site in Liverpool Lawn is a sympathetic intervention which respects the footprint, scale and materials of the surrounding conservation area (Fig 109). Another bright spot is the arches on Military Road which today host a variety of shops and restaurants alongside traditional boat chandlers and workshops (Fig 110). And much media attention has been given to the restoration of the once-derelict Royal Victoria Pavilion and its transformation into the UK's largest branch of JD Wetherspoon when it opened in 2017.

Ramsgate is well placed to exploit the growing phenomenon of food tourism, which offers visitors the taste of a place though speciality restaurants, café culture, farmers' markets, food and drink festivals and 'pop-up' events. Ramsgate could host an open-air market selling locally grown vegetables, beer and wine and celebrating the rich natural resources of the area. This would reconnect the town with its agricultural hinterland. Thanet's climate and the fertility of its land, together with the intensive agricultural methods and the new crops introduced in the 17th and 18th centuries, once created a broad variety of highly prized produce. Hops were once grown in Thanet, as were walnuts, broccoli and asparagus (which still is grown).

Figure 109 (below, right)
This development of seven houses between Liverpool Lawn and Adelaide Gardens (2010–13, Anthony Browne) continues the bow-fronted form and details of Nos 34–35 Liverpool Lawn, terminating in a crenelated block which recalls the sandcastle-like forms of Pier Castle and Townley Castle.
[DP247229]

Figure 110 (below)
Archive is a café and retail space housed within a double-height arch on Military Road. Designed by Haptic Architects, this flexible series of spaces is organised with partitions and fittings of birch plywood.
[Simon Kennedy, Haptic Architects, Archive]

Thanet was also famed for the quality of its malting barley. The strong bottled beer Northdown Ale, mentioned in the mid-17th century diary of Samuel Pepys, was brewed in Thanet using water from a well in Holly Lane in modern day Cliftonville and was widely sold in London as a luxury product. Thanet once abounded in breweries, some long established. Until 1968, Ramsgate was home to what was claimed to be England's oldest brewery, Tomson and Wotton.

Ramsgate harbour has intermittently supported a fishing fleet, with fish being sold on the quay and at purpose-built markets established in 1839 at York Street and in 1880 on the harbour crosswall. Today the fleet is sizable, bringing in sole, skate, plaice, cod and a wide variety of shellfish. Yet little of this catch is sold in Ramsgate. A fish market could be revived as a focal point for residents and visitors, particularly if it was combined with outlets for other local produce and food stalls. And it could supply local restaurants, allowing people to dine in sight of the fishing boats that have delivered the daily catch.

As well as eating the produce of the sea, there are opportunities to celebrate the wonders of the deep, particularly since coastal areas off Ramsgate were designated as marine conservation zones in 2013 and 2019.[159] This stretch of water is a key part of Britain's history and its unique marine archaeology might spur a nomination proposal for this coastal area to be considered for inscription on UNESCO's World Heritage List. The inclusion in 2001 of the Dorset and East Devon Coast has conferred worldwide fame and status on the 'Jurassic Coast' and has boosted the economy of Lyme Regis, the town most associated with it.

On land, recent developments have reinstated the setting of the landscape around Ramsgate. During the 19th century, Pegwell Bay to the south-west of the town was a celebrated beauty spot. William Dyce's strikingly original painting *Pegwell Bay, Kent – a Recollection of October 5th 1858* portrays the painter's family collecting shells, or fossils, while in the background the chalk strata of the cliff are depicted in minute detail and Donati's Comet can be seen crossing the sky (Fig 111). The tranquillity of this place was marred during the 20th century by the construction of Richborough Power Station in 1962–3 and the Pegwell Bay Hoverport in 1969. The latter closed in 1982, its terminal buildings were demolished and the concrete apron is today returning to nature; the power station was demolished in 2012. The special qualities of Pegwell Bay's landscape and ecosystem is recognised by its inclusion in multiple designations including a Site of Special Scientific Interest and a National Nature Reserve.

Figure 111
Pegwell Bay, Kent – a Recollection of October 5th 1858
by William Dyce highlights the natural beauty of the coast around Ramsgate. Based on a trip made in the autumn of 1858, it depicts members of his family gathering shells. Dyce's interest in geology and astronomy is suggested in his rendering of the chalk strata of the cliffs and the trail of Donati's comet, faintly visible in the upper central portion of the painting.
[© Tate, London 2019]

Ramsgate's clifftop parks, on either side of the town centre, deserve to be celebrated as a gift bestowed on the town by far-sighted citizens and previous council administrations. They form a near-continuous, four-mile green swathe which has a high amenity value. Ellington Park, at the back of the town, received a £1.6m Heritage Lottery Fund grant in December 2018. The park sits in the centre of Ramsgate's prime, late 19th-century residential suburb and could be the key to its revival. All these open spaces have a major role to play in the well-being of residents and visitors.

As well as promoting Ramsgate as a place, there can also be a role for trading on links to famous people associated with the town. Charles Dickens and A W N Pugin could be used to market Ramsgate as a way of indicating that it was, and remains, an absorbing place to visit. Dickens' essay 'The Tuggs's at Ramsgate' is a brilliant evocation of a seaside holiday prior to the arrival of the railways and could be one hook to capture a new audience's imagination.

Similarly, the restoration of the Houses of Parliament offers an opportunity to highlight the visionary work of its architect, A W N Pugin, in Ramsgate. Twenty years ago, the core of his Catholic community on the west cliff was at

Figure 112
The entrance hall of A W N Pugin's The Grange, as restored by the Landmark Trust. Note the floor tiles with Pugin's crest, the wallpaper which bears Pugin's family motto 'En Avant' and the distinctive pierced stair balustrade.
[John Miller, courtesy of Landmark Trust]

risk and Pugin was a little-known figure in Ramsgate. St Augustine's Church was seldom open to the public, its roof leaked and the electrics were dangerous. Today, the church is now open daily, its interior has been reordered to restore Pugin's original layout and a Heritage Lottery-funded visitor centre was completed in 2017. Pugin's house, The Grange and St Edward's Presbytery have been restored by the Landmark Trust to the highest conservation standards, and are available all-year round as holiday lets (Fig 112).

In the mid-19th century, Ramsgate gained a reputation as an intellectual 'London-on-Sea', and attracted many cultural and artistic figures. Among these was Sir Moses Montefiore, a key figure in Jewish emancipation (much as Pugin was to Roman Catholicism) who established his own ideal community at Hereson on the east cliff. And although Vincent van Gogh may have only lived briefly in the town, his presence could be used to catch the public's imagination. This deeply talented and troubled artist only ever found positive things to say about Ramsgate.

Conclusion

When, in October 1943, its councillors debated Ramsgate's future, a balance was sought between pressures to reconstruct and a growing desire to preserve the town's special qualities. One councillor commented that 'the characteristics of Ramsgate must be preserved'. When it came to stimulating tourism it was argued that its historic townscape, in all its picturesque irregularity, was not a liability but an asset. 'Ramsgate has got to live by selling holidays', commented another, 'and one thing which people wanted when on holiday was a complete change of surroundings'.[160]

Such wisdom, which was far from universally acknowledged in the middle of the 20th century, could underpin thinking about the town's future. Circumstances may have changed, but striking the balance between preservation/ossification and reconstruction/destruction remains an abiding debate throughout England's historic environment. Ramsgate has a breathtaking setting, a stunning, historic built environment and a highly engaging 'back story'. Challenging national perceptions and raising local expectations are the essential first steps in reviving the town's fortunes. For Ramsgate to be successful, it has to be Ramsgate.

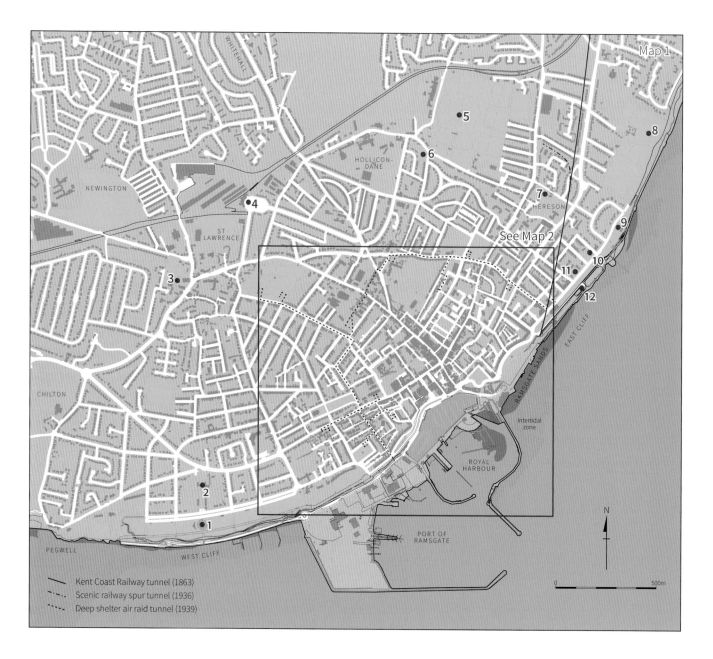

Map 1

See Map 2

WHITEHALL

NEWINGTON

ST LAWRENCE

HOLLICON-DANE

HERESON

CHILTON

PEGWELL

WEST CLIFF

EAST CLIFF

RAMSGATE SANDS

Intertidal zone

ROYAL HARBOUR

PORT OF RAMSGATE

N

—— Kent Coast Railway tunnel (1863)
–·–·– Scenic railway spur tunnel (1936)
········ Deep shelter air raid tunnel (1939)

0   500m

Gazetteer

1 Royal Esplanade, Prince Edward's Promenade and Western Undercliff

This seafront improvement scheme was undertaken in 1924–9 by the Borough of Ramsgate on the former Warre estate. The layout, by Franklin & Deacon of Luton, included a long strip of public gardens and leisure facilities bounded by a promenade and a broad boulevard, Royal Esplanade.

2 Belmont

Belmont was built *c* 1795 for Joseph Ruse as a seaside villa in the Gothick style. Renamed West Cliff House, it was later the residence of the Earl of Darnley and the Warre family, who hosted Princess Victoria in 1836.

3 St Laurence's Church

The Church of St Laurence was founded as a chapel of ease to St Mary at Minster in Thanet. It was assigned to St Augustine's Abbey in 1124 and obtained its own parish in 1275. The aisled nave and tower are of late 12th century date, and the chancel was enlarged in the early 13th century. Restorations were carried out in 1858, 1866 and 1888.

4 Ramsgate Station

Ramsgate Station, which replaced the 1846 Town Station and the 1863 Ramsgate Harbour station, was constructed in 1924–6 by Sir Robert McAlpine and Sons for the Southern Railway. Designed by the 25 year old E Maxwell Fry in a Beaux Arts style, the station's central booking hall is flanked by two lower, angled wings.

5 Ramsgate Cemetery

In 1869 Ramsgate's burial board purchased 20 acres of land north-east of the town. The cemetery layout was devised by A Markham Nesfield, while George Gilbert Scott junior designed the gatehouse, walls, and Anglican and non-conformist mortuary chapels. An eastern extension of 1898 was necessary to provide for the new parishes of St Luke and Holy Trinity.

6 Jewish Cemetery

The Jewish Cemetery was privately established in 1872 by Benjamin Norden for Thanet's Jewish community. It is entered through a brick *ohel* or prayer hall incorporated into the boundary wall. The ground was extended in 1913 and 1931.

7 Montefiore Synagogue and Mausoleum

Founded by (Sir) Moses Montefiore, the synagogue was designed by his cousin David Mocatta and built in 1831–3. The interior was lined with marble in 1912 and further alterations, including stained glass windows, were undertaken in 1933. The adjoining Mausoleum of Sir Moses and Judith, Lady Montefiore is a stuccoed and rusticated structure erected in 1864. It is based upon the Tomb of Rachel outside Bethlehem, whose renovation Montefiore funded.

8 Site of East Cliff Lodge

Intended as a marine villa for Benjamin Bond Hopkins MP, East Cliff Lodge was unfinished at his death in 1794. It was designed in a Tudor Gothic idiom by the Margate surveyor Charles Boncey, along with stables, estate workers' cottages and a gatehouse. In 1831–3 the house was

Stained glass at East Court. [DP262686]

enlarged by Decimus Burton for Sir Moses Montefiore, who installed a vinery manufactured by W and D Bailey of Holborn. The house was demolished in 1953 and its grounds became the King George VI Memorial Park.

9 Winterstoke Gardens

Winterstoke Gardens was funded by Dame Janet Stancomb-Wills at a cost of £10,000 and opened by her in 1923. Designed by Sir John Burnet & Partners, the Italianate garden was laid out by Messrs Pulham & Sons and includes a Pulhamite rock garden, sun shelter-cum- viewing platform and fountain pool. In 1935–6 the adjacent section of cliff was reinforced with a Pulhamite sea wall incorporating a flight of steps descending to an undercliff promenade.

10 East Court

East Court, of 1889–90 by Ernest George and Harold Peto, is a fine example of the vernacular revival style. It was built for the businessman and philanthropist William Henry Wills, first Baron Winterstoke. He bequeathed the house to his adoptive niece, Dame Janet Stancomb-Wills, Ramsgate's benefactor and first woman mayor.

11 Coastguard Station

Ramsgate's coastguard station was erected in 1865–6 to designs by the Admiralty architect Henry Case. Ranged around three sides of a grassed court, the cottages are today private dwellings. The station replaced an early 19th-century watch house on the Sands, cleared to make way for the Kent Coast Railway Company's line.

12 Granville Marina

In 1870 the Board of Trade granted E W Pugin a lease for an inclined drive leading from the Sands to the East Cliff. Works were suspended before Pugin's death but were completed in a revised form in 1876–7 by Edmund F Davis, the new owner of the Granville Hotel. The development included Marina Parade, a parade of shops, tea rooms and houses designed by J T Wimperis.

13 St Augustine's Church, St Edward's Presbytery and The Grange

The Roman Catholic church of St Augustine was founded, funded and designed by A W N Pugin. Intended as the centrepiece of a small Catholic community, the church was built in 1845–51 by the contractor George Myers at a total cost of around £20,000. St Edward's was commenced in 1850 as the presbytery to St Augustine's. The Grange was designed by A W N Pugin for himself and his family and built in 1843–4. Additions and alterations were subsequently carried out by his son E W Pugin. An extensive restoration was completed in 2004–6 for the Landmark Trust.

14 St Augustine's Abbey

A W N Pugin had projected a monastery north of St Augustine's Road but did not live to see it realised. The present south and west ranges were built in 1860–1 by W E Smith to designs by E W Pugin for a Benedictine community. It was joined by the east wing (1904, P P Pugin), the Bergh Memorial Library (1926, C H Purcell) and the north range and west gateway (1934–7, C C Winmill). To the north-west is the site of St Augustine's College (E W Pugin, 1860–1, demolished 1973), originally a house for Alfred Luck, the benefactor of the monastery.

15 Chartham Terrace

This row of five knapped-flint houses was developed in 1850–1 by Matthew Habershon and his son William Gilbee Habershon on part of the former Townley estate.

16 Royal Crescent

The west cliff's counterpart to Wellington Crescent, Royal Crescent was initiated in 1826 by Robert Townley, probably to a design by his mother, Mary Townley. Eight houses had been erected by 1831, when it was agreed that the crescent would be reduced to half its planned length. In 1863 the crescent was completed to its original design by W E Smith. In 1947 several properties were converted to the Regency Hotel.

St Augustine's Church. [DP247165]

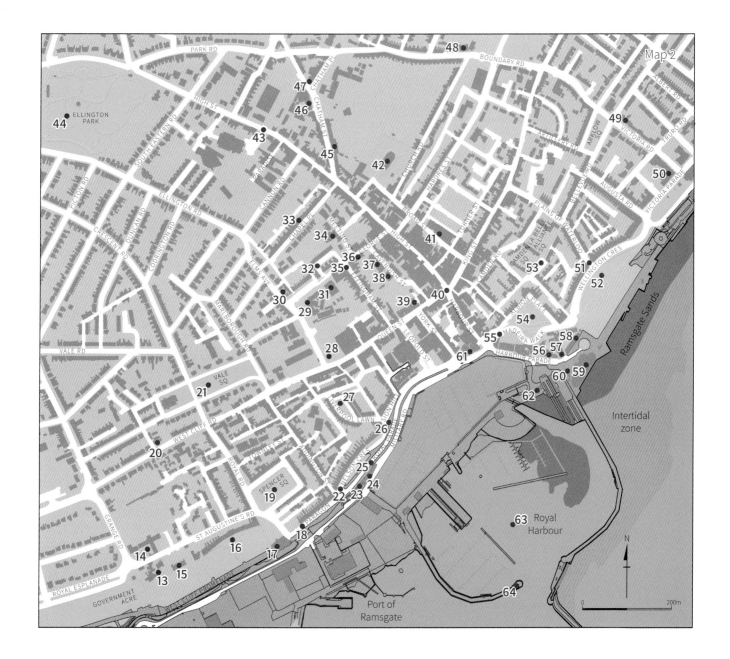

Map 2

44 • ELLINGTON PARK

48

BOUNDARY RD

49

50

47
46
43
45
42

33
34
41
36
32 35 37
38
30
31
29
39 40
51
52
53
28
54
55 58
56 57
61
60 59
21
62
27
26
63 Royal Harbour
20
25
24
19 22 23
16 18
17
14
13 15
64

N

Intertidal zone

Ramsgate Sands

Port of Ramsgate

0   200m

153

17 West Cliff Concert Hall

This 1914 venue was designed by the borough engineer T G Taylor. By sinking the building into the cliff, he was able to incorporate access to a sunken garden to the north and a sea-facing balcony to the south.

18 Paragon

Paragon is a terrace of four-storey houses of variegated appearance. Nos 1–5 were built piecemeal by George Kennard and others from *c* 1800. In 1802, No 3 was rated to George Louch (1746–1811), deputy engineer to Ramsgate harbour. Nos 6–10 were built by Thomas Grundy, James Craven and others on land conveyed to them in 1811 by the broker Moses Lara. Nos 17–22, of *c* 1860, replaced the Isabella Baths (later the Royal Kent Baths) which opened in 1816. They were designed, along with the surviving No 16, by the engineer R S Meikleham.

19 Spencer Square

James Townley acquired the site occupied by the present square between 1798 and 1804, and by February 1800 it was in use as an army barracks. Townley built a terrace of ten houses (35–42 Spencer Square and 1–3 Royal Road), with stables and coach houses behind (today Townley Street). After 1815 the terrace was used as lodging houses, while the remainder of the square was laid out for building in 1836 by G M Hinds. In 1876 Vincent Van Gogh lodged at No 11 while he taught at a boy's school at 6 Royal Road.

20 Seamen's Infirmary

The Seamen's Infirmary was founded in 1848 for the medical treatment and accommodation of 'seamen of all nations brought into the Port of Ramsgate, also for fishermen and residents in Thanet who are too poor to pay for attendance and nursing at their own homes'.[161]

21 Vale Square and Christ Church

The Vale was a speculative development of middle-class houses on land purchased by James Creed Eddels in August 1839. He probably built Victoria Terrace on the east side of an elongated square before developing the remainder of the land as detached and paired villas. The portion west of Crescent Road was owned by Edells's builder, William Saxby senior. In 1846–8 he erected Christ Church, an early work by Sir George Gilbert Scott. Its cost of over £8,000 was met by public subscriptions.

22 Nelson Crescent

This crescent of 19 houses was built piecemeal between about 1799 and 1809 on arable land owned by John Flemming senior. The development included a small pleasure ground and stabling at the rear.

23 Jacob's Ladder

The original Jacob's Ladder was a timber-framed structure completed in 1754. It was said to have been erected by Jacob Steed, perhaps a corruption of the name of the Ramsgate carpenter Joseph Stead who died in 1787 aged 59. It was replaced in 1826 by the existing flight of stone steps designed by John Shaw senior.

24 Sailors' Home and Smack Boys' Home

An initiative of the Revd Eustace Brenan, the Sailors' Home and Harbour Mission was designed by W E Smith and was opened in July 1878 by Marquis Conyngham. Next to it A R Pite designed a hostel in 1880–1 for the apprentices of fishing smacks laid up at the harbour. It closed in 1915.

25 Royal Parade

Royal Parade is an inclined carriageway constructed in 1893–5 to link Harbour Parade with the west cliff. The road is carried on an arcaded retaining wall which fronts Military Road and into which are let a series of chandlers' stores, today used as shops and restaurants.

26 Sion Hill

Sion Hill, a terrace of eight houses adjoined by the Foy Boat Tavern, was developed in the 1790s to serve the booming resort. No 8 was described in 1798 as 'very eligibly situate for letting lodgings'.[162] Outside Sion Hill, a red flag was hoisted on a signal post to indicate 10 or more feet of water in the harbour. A tide ball replaced the flag in the 19th century. Destroyed by enemy action during the Second World War, Nos 3–4, 6–8 and the Foy Boat Tavern were rebuilt as Sion Court, Sion House and the Foy Boat Hotel.

27 Liverpool Lawn

This speculative development was constructed *c* 1827–36 by the Ramsgate builder James Crisford. Nos 1–19 (originally Liverpool Terrace) are gently curved to maximise views of the Harbour, while Nos 24–33 (Liverpool Place) are squeezed in across the lawn. The group is completed by the stuccoed Nos 20–22 which face seaward.

Sailors' Church. [DP247150]

28 Site of Tomson and Wotton brewery

Tomson and Wotton's was the largest and longest established of Ramsgate's several breweries. Probably established in the 16th century, the Queen Street site was purchased in 1680 by Thomas Tomson and remained in the ownership of his family until it was bought out by Whitbread in 1957. In 1867, when Thomas Wotton was taken into partnership, the brewery owned 21 pubs in Ramsgate, Broadstairs and Sandwich. The brewery was redeveloped after closure in 1968 and the site is today a supermarket.

29 Clarendon House Grammar School

Ramsgate's County School was built in 1908–9 for the sum of £11,222 by Kent County Council. Its butterfly plan, devised by the county architect W H Robinson, was intended to accommodate 150 boys and 150 girls in angled wings, with a corner entrance and a rear hall. In 2011, the school merged with the Chatham House Grammar School to become the co-educational Chatham & Clarendon Grammar School.

30 Barber's Almshouses

Opened in September 1899 by the Bishop of Dover, these almshouses were endowed by Frances Barber in memory of her husband and son. Twelve dwellings are ranged around a small courtyard, entered from an ashlar gateway in the Jacobean revival style. Over the central entrance is a niche containing a statue of St George.

31 Public Library

S D Adshead won the 1902 design competition for a technical school and public library but the site was instead divided up and a smaller library was completed in 1904 to Adshead's revised designs. Its pedimented front alone survived a serious fire in 2004.

32 Guildford Lawn

This L-shaped terrace of 19 stuccoed houses with bow fronts was built by William Saxby senior in the early 1840s. Occupying the former garden of Samuel Brimstone, the development was named after the Earl of Guildford, Lord Warden of the Cinque Ports. Lawn Villas replaced the terrace's ornamental garden some time after 1905.

33 Chapel Place

Ramsgate's earliest uniform terrace, Chapel Place was built c 1788–90 by John Horn on land owned by the Ramsgate solicitor John Fagg. The prominent bay windows at No 35 were added c 1886 by Pugin & Pugin for Dr Samuel Woodman JP. Chapel House (built in 1968 as Apollo House) occupies the site of a chapel of ease dedicated to St Mary. Of six bays with a central pediment, the chapel was demolished after being twice bombed in the Second World War.

34 Ebenezer Chapel

Meeting Street takes its name from the Ebenezer Chapel, which was first erected on this site in 1743. It was replaced in 1838–9 by the present chapel, designed by G M Hinds and W Woodland and built by William Saxby senior. It closed in 1978 and is today a nursery.

35 Effingham Street

Effingham Street was laid out off Queen Street in the early 18th century, and was first rated in 1728 as Brick Street. No 20 was rated in 1789 to Rear Admiral William Fox (1733–1810), later passing to his nephew Richard Tomson. In 1901 it was sold to Ramsgate Corporation who in 1905 remodelled it as a fire station. At the top of the street was Effingham House (No 44), possibly built in the 1760s for Richard Cracraft and demolished after the Second World War.

36 St George's Hall

This assembly hall was built in 1848–9 by Edward Bing to a classical design by G M Hinds, whose practice designed new fittings 30 years later. In the 20th century it successively served as a cinema, a furniture warehouse and a snooker club before being converted for residential use.

37 Cavendish Baptist Chapel

This chapel was completed in 1840 at a cost of about £4,000. According to a contemporary account, its interior was 'fitted up in a kind of double theatre, having at each side rising seats, with a row of seats in the centre'.[163] To the north was a British School for boys and girls, replaced in 1900 by a red-brick Sunday school.

38 Cavendish House

Completed c 1840 for the American-born solicitor Lodovick Pollock, Cavendish House featured elaborate gardens and a geometrical stone staircase. After serving as the High School for Girls and the Free Library and Technical Institute, in 1929 it was remodelled as Ramsgate Police Station. A magistrates' court, added to the south in 1966, has been demolished.

39 1–2 Queen's Court

Of probable late 17th-century origin, 1–2 Queen's Court is of two-and-a-half storeys of knapped and coursed flint, with casement windows set under shallow brick arches. It may originally have been approached from Queen Street via a forecourt, later encroached upon by 21–23 Queen Street.

40 Former Marketplace

The crossroads of Ramsgate's four principal streets was known as the Sole, after the Kentish term for a watering place or pond. A market house was erected here under the provisions of an Act of Parliament of 1785. In 1839 it was replaced with a town hall raised on a colonnade over a market, in turn demolished in 1955. 1–7 Queen Street opposite (1894–5, architects Stenning & Jennings of Canterbury for Hammond &

Co's Canterbury Bank) occupies the site of a circulating library and bank built c 1808 for Peter Burgess. The former Midland Bank of 1921 at 1–3 High Street replaced the London Hotel, established by William Thompson in 1789.

41 St James's Hall

St James's Hall occupies the site of the Ramsgate Theatre, opened in 1825 by Faucet Saville, who ran theatres at Margate and Greenwich. Rebuilt after a fire in 1829 and overhauled in 1861, it was used for a variety of purposes, including auctions, entertainments and public lectures.

42 St George's Church

St George's was built in 1825–7 to a design by Henry Hemsley junior, revised by H E Kendall. Of white Ipswich bricks with bath stone dressings, the church is dominated by a lofty west tower surmounted by an octagonal lantern. Outside is a war memorial by Herbert Baker, dedicated by the Archbishop of Canterbury in October 1920.

43 'Westminster'

The upper part of High Street (formerly West Street) was known as Westminster. Present on Lewis's 1736 map are the house of Capt Thomas Abbot (No 146, demolished), the Eagle Inn at the junction of Windmill Hill, and the ropewalk which became Cannon Street. Nos 127–135, No 125 and Monkton House (No 124) opposite combine polite Georgian fronts with shaped gables.

St George's Church. [DP247214]

44 Ellington Park

Ramsgate's first municipal park, Ellington Park opened in September 1893 at a cost of £12,400. J Cheal & Sons of Crawley laid out a picturesque layout which featured serpentine paths, specimen trees, an ornamental fountain and a rustic bandstand. The park occupies the grounds of the demolished Ellington House, the seat of a freehold farm of medieval origin.

45 Chatham House School

The school traces its origins to 1796, when the schoolmaster William Humble purchased the three-storey Chatham House on Love Lane, today Chatham Street. He carried out several improvements and erected two school houses. The present red-brick range of 1879–82 was designed by Aaron Twyman for the headmaster and owner E G Banks. From 1922 the school was maintained by Kent County Council as the Chatham House County School for Boys. The Redman Wing, a science block and sports hall, opened in 1962 on the former Townley Castle site.

46 Townley House

Completed in 1792, Townley House was designed by Mary Townley as a family residence. The exterior is dominated by a central bow front incorporating statues of artificial Coade stone. Townley House was the holiday residence of the Duchess of Kent and Princess Victoria for several seasons in the 1820s, and from 1835 was occupied by a ladies' boarding school.

47 Chatham Place

Nos 1–5 were built between about 1790 and 1802; they have relatively uniform stock brick facades but different plot widths. No 1 was rated at £1 to John Horn in 1794; by 1798 it was owned by James Townley. No 4, a double-pile house of four storeys, was built *c* 1801 for the Canterbury printer and bookseller James Saffery. Chatham Place was until 1889 a cul-de sac.

48 Gasworks offices

A gasworks was established in 1824 by the Isle of Thanet Gas Light and Coke Company at the junction of Hardres Street and Boundary Road. By 1872 the site had been extended north of Boundary Road. In 1877 the company was acquired by Ramsgate's local board which further enlarged the site. A red-brick and terracotta office building with a prominent central tower was added in 1899–1900.

49 Mount Albion House

In origin, 22–24 Victoria Road are two late 18th-century dwellings, converted *c* 1807 into Mount Albion House for Lady Augusta Murray. Between 1807 and 1809 she acquired about 16 acres of adjoining land with an approach from King Street. The estate was developed from 1838 to a layout by the London architect Thomas Allason.

50 Granville Hotel

The centrepiece of E W Pugin's projected St Lawrence-on-Sea development, the Granville opened in 1869, catering for health-conscious guests with a suite of saltwater spa baths. It was accompanied by a promenade and bridleway, which later became Victoria Gardens, and a sunken garden used in the winter as a skating rink. Updated in 1900 by the architect Horace Field, the Granville was converted to flats in 1948 and has remained in residential use.

51 Wellington Crescent

Bisected by the contemporaneous Plains of Waterloo, Wellington Crescent is a development of 1818–24 by James Underdown, William Miller, James Smith and Pilcher Longley. Smith and Miller built detached houses for themselves, respectively Waterloo Cottage (50 Plains of Waterloo) and East Cliff House (*c* 1844 by G M Hinds).

52 East Cliff Bandstand

The centrepiece of Wellington Crescent Gardens was initially occupied by an oak statue of the Duke of Wellington, erected by William Miller. In 1914 the Empire Bandstand was moved to this spot from Victoria Gardens. It was replaced in 1939 with a distinctive domed bandstand, accompanied by a surfaced open-air dance floor.

53 Camden Square / La Belle Alliance Square

The layout of these two squares of lower-middle-class houses was dictated by field boundaries and a road laid out in 1833 from Clover Hill to Plains of Waterloo. In 1835, Camden Place (1–12 La Belle Alliance Square) was cited by one commentator as an example of a 'mania for building' at Ramsgate.[164]

54 Albion Place and Gardens

Albion Place, an L-shaped terrace overlooking the harbour, was Ramsgate's first large-scale seafront development. It was developed from 1789 by Stephen Heritage, the innkeeper of the King's Head Tavern, who sold off 28 plots together with a covenant to ensure a regular façade. Albion House, of *c* 1794 for the Canterbury alderman James Simmons, occupies a double plot at the east end. It hosted many titled visitors to Ramsgate including the Archbishop of Canterbury and Princess Victoria. Initially laid out as a residents' pleasure ground, Albion Place Gardens was altered with the erection of Madeira Walk in the 1890s.

55 Madeira Walk

With Royal Parade, Madeira Walk of 1892–3 was the centrepiece of a municipal development which improved access to suburban development on the east and west cliffs. Laid out on a meandering path along the edge of Albion Place Gardens, Madeira Walk incorporates rock gardens and a picturesque waterfall formed from Pulhamite artificial stone.

56 Custom House

Built in 1894–5 for a cost of £3,800 by the Margate contractors Paramor & Sons, the custom house formed part of a programme of seafront improvement works overseen by the borough engineer W A McIntosh Valon. It replaced Samuel Wyatt's pier house of 1802.

57 Pier Castle, 94–98 Harbour Parade

Pier Castle was completed in 1818 for the Townley family, and was probably rented to bathing machine proprietors and their employees. Later used as a seaside restaurant, the structure was rendered in cement in 1930.

58 100–114 Harbour Parade

Nos 100–108 occupy the site of early bathing rooms, replaced c 1836 with the classical Victoria Baths. A variety of saloons, dining rooms, music halls and bazaars traded here in the Victorian period. Nos 110–114 was rebuilt by the brewer Tomson and Wotton in 1936 as The Refectory. To the north is Kent Terrace, developed in 1833–7 after the chalk outcrop was cut back.

59 Royal Victoria Pavilion

An early work by S D Ashead, the Royal Victoria Pavilion of 1903 provided entertainment facilities and enhanced the approach to Ramsgate Sands. Later converted for use as a cinema, casino and nightclub, the 'Pav' re-opened in 2017 as a Wetherspoon's pub.

60 Obelisk

This granite obelisk commemorates the embarkation and safe return of King George IV in 1821. Designed by John Shaw senior, it was erected in 1822–3 and bears inscriptions in Latin and English.

61 Royal Sailors' Rest

The Royal Sailors' Rest was erected in 1903 by the British and Foreign Sailors' Society as a seamen's hostel and bethel. Its architect, A R Pite, had earlier designed the Smack Boys' Home. The Sailors' Rest closed in 1919 and was later used as a hotel.

62 Clock House

This classical clock house was completed c 1816 by John Shaw senior. The lower flanking wings housed a warehouse and a carpenter's workshop. For many years the building served as the Ramsgate Maritime Museum.

63 Harbour

Work on a new harbour commenced in 1750. A cross wall and inner basin, added in 1776–9 by the civil engineer John Smeaton, was intended to create a head of water to scour the outer harbour. Later additions include an extension to the east pier head, also by Smeaton (1787), a dry dock (1808–9) and slipways (1838–9 and later).

64 Lighthouse

Designed in 1841 by John Shaw junior, this Cornish granite structure replaced a lighthouse of 1794–5 by Samuel Wyatt situated nearer the pier head.

65 Deep tunnel shelters

Ramsgate's air raid precautions scheme, devised in 1939 by the borough engineer R D Brimmell, included a circuit of tunnel shelters excavated at an average depth of around 18m. Entered from 23 entrances situated in residential areas, the tunnels included a ventilation system, chemical toilets and first aid posts.

Notes

1   Anon 1846, 18.

2   Manson *et al* 2018.

3   Small 2019.

4   Last 2019.

5   van Gogh, Vincent 1876 Letter of 6 May to Theo van Gogh, http://www.vangoghletters.org/vg/letters/let081/letter.html [accessed 11 April 2019].

6   Lewis 1723, 123.

7   Anon 1809, 3.

8   Cobbett 1853, 253.

9   Boys 1792, 528–9.

10   Leland 1909, 61.

11   Camden 1806, 316.

12   Ibid.

13   Lewis 1723, 124.

14   *The Kentish Post, or Canterbury News Letter*, 22–25 May 1754, 1.

15   Hull 1955, 174.

16   Dickens 1836, 9.

17   Kent History and Library Centre (KHLC), R/U2446/F1, family holiday journal of Francis James Hawkins, entry of 7 August 1828.

18   *Kentish Weekly Post*, 8 October 1802, 4.

19   Canterbury Cathedral Archives (CCA), DCC/AddMS/271/1, Daniel Benham, 'Journal of an excursion to Ramsgate in July and August 1829', entry of 20 July 1829.

20   *Kentish Gazette*, 25 March 1769, 1.

21   *London Courier and Evening Gazette*, 24 September 1801, 3.

22   *Kentish Gazette*, 6 August 1768, 2.

23   Anon *c* 1789, 30.

24   William Cowper, letter of July 1779 to William Unwin, in Southey 1853, 231.

25   'T G' 1763, 23.

26   Thomas Gray, letter of 15 February 1767 to the Revd William Mason, in Mitford 1853, 375.

27   Hull 1955, 174.

28   Cozens 1793, 49–50.

29   *Kentish Gazette*, 10 June 1775, 1.

30   *Kentish Gazette*, 14 August 1776, 1.

31   Carey 1799, 40–1.

32   *Journals of the House of Commons*, vol. 40, 22 February 1785, 552–3.

33   *An Act for better paving, cleansing, repairing, lighting, and watching the highways, streets and lanes of and in the vill of Ramsgate, in the county of Kent; and for removing and preventing annoyances therein, and for erecting a market-house, and holding a public markt in the said vill*, 25 Geo. III, c. 34.

34   KHLC, RA/AM3/1/1, Minutes of the proceedings of the Ramsgate Improvement Commissioners, 9 July 1785.

35   Ibid, 14 May 1791.

36   Ibid, 7 December 1785.

37   *Bath Chronicle and Weekly Gazette*, 18 September 1766, 3.

38 Richardson 1885, 146.

39 Seymour 1776, 652–4.

40 *Kentish Gazette*, 10 August 1768, 2.

41 Richardson 1885, 195.

42 Ramsgate Library Local History Collection (RLLHC): R/TR2188/2, Coke journal, entry of 28 July 1788.

43 Queen Victoria's Journals, vol. 12, 30 September 1836, at http://www.queenvictoriasjournals.org/search/displayItemFromId.do?FormatType=fulltextimgsrc&QueryType=articles&ItemID=18360930 [accessed 11 April 2019].

44 'TG' 1763, 5–6.

45 *Derby Mercury*, 8 August 1760, 4.

46 Southey 1853, 231.

47 'TG' 1763, 14.

48 'Slenderwit' 1798, 1.

49 *The Times*, 3 February 1804, 3.

50 *Kentish Gazette*, 12 March 1799, 4.

51 CCA, U3-19/11/A/13, rate books, assessment of 12 August 1808.

52 National Army Museum, 1968/07/177/7–8, letter of 9 August 1809 from General Alex Hope to Lt Gen Sir George Nugent.

53 *Kentish Gazette*, 26 September 1797, 4.

54 *Kentish Weekly Post,* 22 December 1815, 5.

55 CCA, U3-19/11/A/18, rate books, assessment of 11 June 1818.

56 Martin 1832, 28.

57 Anon 1824, 18.

58 *Kentish Weekly Post*, 25 May 1821, 1.

59 Anon 1861, 132.

60 RLLHC: R/TR2188/1, Porden diary, entry of 9 August 1820.

61 KHLC, R/U2446/F1, Hawkins journal, entry of 21 August 1828.

62 RLLHC: R/TR2188/1, Porden diary, entry of 20 July 1820.

63 *Kentish Gazette*, 9 September 1834, 3.

64 *Morning Post*, 14 September 1816, 4.

65 *Kentish Weekly Post*, 17 September 1802, 4.

66 RLLHC: R/TR2188/2, Coke journal, entry of 6 August 1788.

67 *Kentish Weekly Post*, 7 August 1807, 4.

68 Anon 1853, 307.

69 CCA, DCC/AddMS/271/1, Daniel Benham, 'Journal of an excursion to Ramsgate in July and August 1829', entry of 20 July 1829.

70 Dickens 1836, 7–8.

71 Fussell 1818, 115.

72 Samuel Taylor Coleridge, letter of 28 October 1822 to James Gillman, in Whyman, 1985, 116.

73 KHLC, R/U774/T17, agreement of 6 October 1841 by Edward Lewis concerning schoolhouse at Albion Mews.

74 Williams 1893, 174.

75 Chapman 1954, 380.

76 KHLC, R/U774/T134, lease and release of 2/3 March 1791.

77 Campbell 1969, 159.

78 The National Archives, PROB 11/1910/74, Mary Townley, will of 16 April 1839.

79 The Repertory of Arts, Manufactures, and Agriculture, vol. 17, 1810, p.191.

80 Select Committee on Foreign Trade 1822, 276.

81 Ireland 1828, 545.

82 *Kentish Times and Farmers' Gazette*, 4 May 1839, 4.

83 *Canterbury Journal, Kentish Times and Farmers' Gazette*, 13 July 1839, 3.

84 Osborne 1835, 32.

85 Anon 1809, 109.

86 *Dover Telegraph*, 2 September 1848, 1.

87 Smith 1846, 235.

88 Stone 1846, 298.

89 Anon 1869, 3.

90 *Canterbury Journal*, 30 May 1857, 3.

91 *Thanet Advertiser*, 10 October 1868, 2.

92 *Thanet Advertiser*, 15 May 1869, 1.

93 *Thanet Advertiser*, 30 September 1876, 3.

94 *Thanet Advertiser*, 28 July 1883, 3.

95 G L 1858, 32.

96 Smith 2012, 7.

97 *South Eastern Gazette*, 24 January 1865, 5.

98 *Thanet Advertiser*, 10 November 1866, 2.

99 *Thanet Advertiser*, 16 May 1891, 2.

100 Festing 1988, 99.

101 Busson 1985, 111.

102 *West Kent Guardian*, 1 September 1849, 6.

103 *Thanet Advertiser*, 23 November 1878, 3.

104 'Report of the Lancet Sanitary Commission on English Watering Places: Ramsgate', *The Lancet*, 19 August 1876, 258–9.

105 *Thanet Advertiser*, 17 December 1859, 1.

106 *The Builder*, vol 42, 7 January 1882, 23.

107 Anon 1847.

108 *Dover Telegraph*, 7 May 1853, 1; *Whitstable Times*, 5 November 1887, 5.

109 *Thanet Advertiser*, 15 September 1917, 2; ibid, 24 June 1922, 2.

110 Hill 2007, 292.

111 Ibid, 433.

112 *Thanet Advertiser*, 28 December 1872, 3.

113 *Thanet Advertiser*, 23 August 1902, 8.

114 *Thanet Advertiser*, 3 May 1929, 7.

115 *Thanet Advertiser*, 20 July 1878, 3.

116 *Thanet Advertiser*, 6 November 1880, 3.

117 *Thanet Advertiser*, 18 September 1869, 3.

118 Walker 1877, 804.

119 *South Eastern Gazette*, 8 October 1850, 5.

120 Stamp may have been introduced to Ramsgate by his predecessor, Daniel Benham, who kept a diary of his excursions to Ramsgate.

121 *South Eastern Gazette*, 13 May 1845, 5.

122 *Kentish Gazette*, 7 August 1838, 1.

123 *South Eastern Gazette*, 15 April 1862, 5.

124 *Thanet Advertiser*, 12 June 1869, 3.

125 CCA, U3-19/11/a/19, rate books, assessment of 9 April 1819.

126 Anon 1870, 182. The article can be attributed with reasonable certainty to Seddon on the basis of its correlation to Seddon's *Ancient Examples of Domestic Architecture in the Isle of Thanet* (1872).

127 *Thanet Advertiser*, 22 December 1866, 3.

128 *Thanet Advertiser*, 22 November 1872, 2.

129 *Thanet Advertiser*, 19 May 1866, 1.

130 *Thanet Advertiser*, 2 March 1878, 1.

131 *Thanet Advertiser*, 14 August 1880, 2.

132 Powers 1981, 116.

133 *Thanet Advertiser*, 12 September 1930, 7.

134 *Thanet Advertiser*, 12 December 1930, 5.

135 Hannen Swaffer, 'The New England—but the Old Ramsgate', *Daily Herald*, 3 August 1931, 6.

136 *Thanet Advertiser*, 15 July 1938, 8.

137 Burrows 2017, 31.

138 *Thanet Advertiser*, 19 November 1937, 3.

139 *Thanet Advertiser*, 10 July 1936, 10.

140 *Thanet Advertiser*, 2 August 1929, 5.

141 Powers 1981, 116.

142 *Thanet Advertiser*, 1 April 1938, 6.

143 *Thanet Advertiser*, 16 August 1919, 6.

144 Siminson 1919, unpaginated.

145 Jarman 2010.

146 *Thanet Advertiser*, 24 May 1940, 1.

147 Cited in http://dunkirk1940.org/index.php?&p=1_365 [accessed 11 April 2019].

148 1 & 2 Geo. VI, c. 70.

149 *Thanet Advertiser*, 4 January 1946, 5.

150 *Thanet Advertiser*, 24 March 1944, 1.

151 *Thanet Advertiser*, 20 November 1945, 3.

152 Demetriadi 1997, 59.

153 Stafford and Yates 1985, 169.

154 Select Committee on Regenerating Seaside Towns and Communities 2019, 3. https://publications.parliament.uk/pa/ld201719/ldselect/ldseaside/320/320.pdf [accessed 1 August 2019].

155 Ibid, 10.

156 https://www.gov.uk/government/statistics/english-indices-of-deprivation-2019 [accessed 22 January 2020]; http://dclgapps.communities.gov.uk/imd/iod_index.html# [accessed 22 January 2020].

157 https://www.retailgazette.co.uk/blog/2019/02/footfall-0-7-january-marking-14th-consecutive-month-decline/ [accessed 22 May 2019].

158 https://www.kentlive.news/news/kent-news/how-thanets-businesses-feel-high-2229516 [accessed 22 May 2019].

159 https://www.gov.uk/government/collections/marine-conservation-zone-designations-in-england [accessed 22 May 2019].

160 *Thanet Advertiser*, 8 October 1943, 1.

161 *Thanet Advertiser*, 27 November 1926, 4.

162 *Kentish Gazette*, 20 April 1798, 1.

163 *The Civil Engineer and Architect's Journal*, vol. 3, October 1840, 362–3.

164 *Dover Telegraph*, 24 January 1835, 8.

References and further reading

Anon c 1789 *The New Margate and Ramsgate Guide.* London: H Turpin

Anon 1809 *Picture of Margate.* Margate: Bousfield & Co

Anon 1824 *A Guide to all the Watering and Sea Bathing Places in England and Wales.* London: Longman, Hurst, Rees, Orme and Brown

Anon 1846 *A Practical Guide to the Watering and Sea-Bathing Places on the Coasts of Kent, Sussex and Hampshire.* London: Cradock & Co

Anon 1847 *Second Annual Report of Dumpton Hall School.* London: B W Gardiner

Anon 1853 'The sea-side resorts of the Londoners'. *Chambers's Edinburgh Journal*, 515, 12 November 1853, 305–9

Anon 1861 *A Guide to the Healthiest and Most Beautiful Watering Places in the British Islands.* London: A & C Black

Anon 1869 'Ramsgate Sands'. *Dover Express*, 13 August 1869

Anon 1870 'Sundry buildings in the Isle of Thanet'. *The Building News*, 2 September 1870, 164–5, 9 September 1870, 181–2, 200, 218

Blaker, Catriona 2003 *Edward Pugin and Kent: His Life and Work Within the County.* Ramsgate: Pugin Society

Boys, William 1792 *Collections for an History of Sandwich in Kent: with Notices of the other Cinque Ports and Members, and of Richborough.* Canterbury: Simmons, Kirkby and Jones

Burrows, Jon 2017 *The British Cinema Boom, 1909–1914: A Commercial History.* London: Palgrave Macmillan

Busson, Charles 1985 *The Book of Ramsgate.* Buckingham: Barracuda Books

Camden, William 1806 *Britannia.* London: John Stockdale

Campbell, R 1969 *London Tradesman.* First published in 1747. Newton Abbot: David & Charles

Carey, George Saville 1799 *The Balnea.* London: W West *et al*

Chapman, R W (ed) 1954 *The Works of Jane Austen*, **6**: Minor Works. Oxford: Oxford University Press

Clayson, Allan 2001 *Wish You Were Here: Coleridge's Holidays at Ramsgate 1819–1833.* Ramsgate: A & C Clayson

Cobbett, William 1853 *Rural Rides* …. London: A. Cobbett

Cotton, Charles 1895 *The History and Antiquities of the Church and Parish of St Lawrence, Thanet, in the county of Kent.* London: Simpkin, Marshall, Hamilton, Kent & Co

Cozens, Zechariah 1793 *A Tour though the Isle of Thanet* …. London: J Nichols

Demetriadi, Julian 1997 'The golden years: English seaside resorts 1950–1974', in Shaw, G and Williams, A (eds) *The Rise and Fall of British Coastal Resorts: Cultural and Economic Perspectives.* London: Mansell, 49–75

Dickens, Charles 1836 'The Tuggs's at Ramsgate', *The Library of Fiction, or Family Storyteller* **1**. London: Chapman and Hall, 1–18

Festing, Sally 1988 'Great credit upon the ingenuity and taste of Mr Pulham'. *Garden History* **16** (1), 90–102

Fussell, L 1818 *A Journey Round the Coast of Kent.* London: Baldwin, Cradock and Joy

G L 1858. 'Sea-side photography'. *Photographic News* **1** (3), 24 September.

Hill, Rosemary 1999 *Pugin and Ramsgate.* Ramsgate: Pugin Society

Hill, Rosemary 2007 *God's Architect: Pugin and the Building of Romantic Britain.* New Haven: Yale University Press

Hull, F 1955 'A tour into Kent, 1759'. *Archaeologia Cantiana* **69**, 171–8

Ireland, William Henry 1828 *England's Topographer, or a New and Complete History of the County of Kent*. London: George Virtue

Jarman, C 2010 *Site of the Former Ellington Girls' School, Ellington Place, Ramsgate, Kent: Air Raid Shelter Survey, Documentary and Graffiti Survey Report*. Canterbury Archaeological Trust, report no.2010/64

Last, Jonathan 2019 *Prehistory, Landscape and Heterotopia: a Contribution to the Ramsgate*. HAZ, Historic England research report 24/2019

Leland, John 1909 *The Itinerary of John Leland in Or about the Years 1535–1543*. Edited by Lucy Toulmin Smith. London: George Bell

Lewis, John 1723 *The History and Antiquities Ecclesiastical and Civil of the Isle of Tenet in Kent*. London. 2 edn (1736)

Manson, Diana *et al* 2018 *Ramsgate, Kent: Historic Characterisation of Ramsgate*. Historic England research report 48/2018

Martin, Kennett Beacham 1832 *Oral Traditions of the Cinque Ports and their Localities*. London: W Harding

Matkin, Robert B 1976 'The construction of Ramsgate harbour'. *Transactions of the Newcomen Society* **48** (1), 53–72

Mitford, John (ed) 1853 *The Correspondence of Thomas Gray and William Mason*. London: Richard Bentley

Newman, John 2013 *Kent: North East and East*. New Haven: Yale University Press

Osborne, R C 1835 *New Margate Guide*. Margate

Powers, Alan 1981 '"Architects I have known": The architectural career of S.D. Adshead'. *Architectural History* **24**, 103–23, 160–4

Richardson, Christopher Thomas 1885 *Fragments of History Pertaining to the Vill, Ville or Liberty of Ramsgate*. Ramsgate: Fuller & Co

Robinson, J M 1973 'Samuel Wyatt at Ramsgate'. *Architectural History* **54**, 54–9, 95–6

Select Committee Appointed to Consider of the Means of Improving and Maintaining the Foreign Trade of the Country 1822 *Lights, Harbour Dues, and Pilotage*. London: House of Commons

Select Committee on Regenerating Seaside Towns and Communities 2019 *The Future of Seaside Towns*. London: House of Lords

Seymour, Charles 1776 *A New Topographical, Historical, and Commercial Survey of the Cities, Towns, and Villages of the County of Kent*. Canterbury

Siminson, A H 1919 *Ramsgate During the Great War, 1914–1918*. St Lawrence: A H Siminson

Slenderwit, Simkin [pseud] 1798 *The Sea-Side, a Poem*, 2 edn. London: T N Longman and J Bell.

Small, Fiona and Barber, Martyn 2019 *Ramsgate Heritage Action Zone: An Assessment of Aerial Photographs and Lidar Images*. Historic England research report 25/2019

Smith, Albert 1846 'Tracts for the trains: No 14 Ramsgate, its resources and prospects'. *Illustrated London News*, 10 October 1846, 235

Smith, Joanna 2012 *Coastguard Stations: Introductions to Heritage Assets*. Swindon: English Heritage

Southey, Robert (ed) 1853 *The Works of William Cooper* **2**. London: H G Bohn

Stafford, Felicity and Yates, Nigel (eds) 1985 *The Later Kentish Seaside*. Gloucester: Alan Sutton

Stamp, Gavin 1998 'Ramsgate cemetery chapel'. *Architectural History* **41**, 273–7

Stone, Elizabeth 1846 *Chronicles of Fashion: English Society, from the time of Queen Elizabeth to the Present Day*: **2**. London: Richard Bentley

'T G' 1763 *A Description of the Isle of Thanet, and Particularly of the Town of Margate*. London: J Newbery and W Bristow

Walker, Patricius [pseud] 1877 'Rambles: in Thanet'. *Fraser's Magazine* **16** (96) 792–806

Whyman, John 1985, *The Early Kentish Seaside (1736–1840)*. Gloucester: Alan Sutton

Williams, Montagu 1893 *Round London: Down East and Up West*. London: Macmillan & Co 1893

Informed Conservation Series

This popular Historic England series highlights the special character of some of our most important historic areas and the development of the pressures they are facing. There are over 30 titles in the series, some of which look at whole towns such as Bridport, Coventry and Margate or distinctive urban districts, such as the Jewellery Quarter in Birmingham and Ancoats in Manchester, while others focus on particular building types in a particular place. A few are national in scope focusing, for example, on English school buildings and garden cities.

The purpose of the series is to raise awareness of the interest and importance of aspects of the built heritage of towns and cities undergoing rapid change or large-scale regeneration. A particular feature of each book is a final chapter that focuses on conservation issues, identifying good examples of the re-use of historic buildings and highlighting those assets or areas for which significant challenges remain.

As accessible distillations of more in-depth research, they also provide a useful resource for heritage professionals tackling, as many of the books do, places and building types that have not previously been subjected to investigation from the historic environment perspective. As well as providing a lively and informed discussion of each subject, the books also act as advocacy documents for Historic England and its partners in protecting historic places and keeping them alive for current and future generations.

More information on each of the books in the series and on forthcoming titles can be found on the Historic England website.

HistoricEngland.org.uk